WHEN YOUR PARENT DIES

When Your Parent Dies

A concise and practical source of help and advice for adults grieving the death of a parent

CATHLEEN L. CURRY

AVE MARIA PRESS   Notre Dame, Indiana 46556

© 1993 by Ave Maria Press, Notre Dame, IN 46556

International Standard Book Number: 0-87793-511-4

Library of Congress Catalog Card Number: 93-71436

Cover and text design by Katherine Robinson Coleman

Cover photograph by Justin A. Soleta

Printed and bound in the United States of America.

Acknowledgments

Thanks to Jim Sherman, spiritual director for Shaare Zion Synagogue in Sioux City, IA and to Sr. Jean Beringer, Briar Cliff College, in Sioux City.

Special thanks go to my daughter, Julie Curry, Early Childhood Special Education Consultant, Iowa A.E.A. who assisted in the contents and critiqued the chapter on children; and to my editor at Ave Maria Press, Frank Cunningham, who prodded, poked, encouraged and affirmed as we worked to make this book more focused and readable.

To my father and mother

Arthur and Loretta Linahan

who gave me life

and taught me how

to live and love.

Contents

Introduction

There is a season for everything, a time for every occupation under heaven:

> A time for giving birth,
> a time for dying;
> a time for planting,
> a time for uprooting what has been planted . . .
> a time for knocking down,
> a time for building.
> A time for tears,
> a time for laughter; . . .
> A time for searching,
> a time for losing;
> a time for keeping,
> a time for discarding . . .
> a time for keeping silent,
> a time for speaking.
> A time for loving,
> a time for hating;
> a time for war,
> a time for peace.
>
> *—Ecclesiastes 3:1-8*

Perhaps Qoheleth, the author of Ecclesiastes, did not have the death of a parent in mind when he wrote these words, but they surely echoed my ambivalent feelings at the time of my father's death. Grieving is a time of mixed-up feelings, "A time for giving birth, a time for dying."

Because my father died just one year after my husband's death, I felt as if the whole world had fallen on my shoulders. And like many of us who were mourning

9

twenty years ago, I shoved my feelings down inside and did not deal with them for many years. I carried a heavy load of grief. Although I didn't realize it, this was my "time for dying." After I became involved with a grief group, which taught me how to deal with my loss, I was able to take the lessons I had learned and use them to mourn for both men. My group experience gave me permission to close the door on my past and open a new door to my future. I was able to move from "a time of dying" to "a time for giving birth" to a new me.

I can now see that it was dad's time for dying. For many years he had suffered from Parkinson's disease, a degenerative brain disorder which caused muscle rigidity and tremors. He was seventy-eight years old and was ready to go to his God. I knew this instinctively, although we had never discussed his illness. Death was one of those topics that was never brought up within the family.

Almost ten years earlier dad had taken me to see a sunset at Lands' End in San Francisco, and we had talked about each person's obligation to choose his or her own road in life. Substantially, this is what he wanted me to know:

> Since we have been given free will, we are responsible for our own soul. In making life's decisions, we are expected to listen to what our God is telling us. We hear his word through prayer, the teachings of our parents and the church, and reading as much as we can on the newest scientific discoveries. After analyzing all this, acknowledging our special talents and abilities, and praying that God will guide us to do his will, we decide on which path to follow. Each one of us is called in a unique and special way to make our own decision. It is easy to follow rules and regulations from others, relying on the decisions they have made. But that is not what God has asked us to do. When Jesus told Matthew to "come, follow me," he did

not say, "Ask around and see what the rest are doing." The decision was up to Matthew alone.

Dad explained that he had prayed and spent much time finding God's will over the past years. "Cathy, you'll have to do the same. I have decided that the Catholic church is the way for me. You will have to decide for yourself."

I was past thirty when this conversation took place. I had gone to a Catholic parochial school for thirteen years, was married and had seven children, and I had always thought I had to follow every hierarchical pronouncement word for word. I was one bewildered woman (little girl?)! My father's words gave me permission to think and make decisions for myself. I wasn't able to absorb all that change in one big leap, so I just tucked the information away until it was time to use it.

Several years after dad's death I knew the time had come to use his advice. It was now "a time for uprooting what had been planted." Actually, I didn't need to uproot as much as I needed to sort out and transplant! I needed to answer some questions, form my own conscience, set my own goals, and continue on my journey in a direction that I, with the help of God, had chosen.

Perhaps the death of your parent will be a good time for you to reflect on your past and see what childhood life patterns you are still following in your adult life. Our human nature includes a God-given freedom to choose different and fresh ways of looking at our approach to life. With this freedom to choose, we also must accept the accompanying responsibility of reflecting on the rightness or wrongness of our actions. The death of a parent can be one of those turnaround points. You can choose to change from the negative, compulsive, and addictive actions you acquired as a child to a more positive, life-giving, and loving behavior.

Our mixed-up feelings at the death of a parent can include depression, loneliness, hate, abandonment, love, anger, and relief. Just as Ecclesiastes tells us, this is "a time for loving, a time for hating." In Chapter One we will identify those feelings as well as our actions and the masks that we wear in order to keep our grief a "private affair."

Grief not only affects our emotions, but also our bodily and spiritual health. The foods we eat, the exercise and amount of rest we get have a definite influence on our emotional and spiritual health. In Chapter Two we will look at the first steps we must take to recover from this shock in our lives—practical things we can do to help us through this trauma.

There have been many studies on death in the last twenty years. Research has shown us that any time a loved one dies we experience grief. Swiss psychiatrist Elisabeth Kubler-Ross, a pioneer researcher on death and dying, has outlined five stages of grief that we must work through in order to get on with life. In Chapter Three I discuss some of the tools that helped me to identify the stages of grief in myself. I also discuss grief and growth groups which offer support from the experience of the same hurt and pain.

This bereavement period is one in which we decide what to keep and what to throw away. When we lose our father or mother, there is not only the grief of losing a loved one, but there is another feeling deep within us that asks: "What are my roots? How did my mother/father influence my life? Why am I who I am today? Am I happy with the person I am today? Do I want to stay this way? What part of this do I want to keep? What part do I want to let go? How can I change?" It can be "a time for searching and a time for losing."

In Chapter Four we will spend some time looking at our family of origin and answering some of those questions. We will talk about silence in the family, the unwritten rules and topics that we were forbidden to discuss. These may include sex, death, pregnancy before marriage, retarded or handicapped children, physical, verbal, and emotional abuse, and incest. We will talk about feelings that were to be hidden and never discussed: envy, jealousy, depression, anger, and of course, sexual feelings. Hopefully, our "time for keeping silent" will change to "a time of speaking."

We will look at some of the newer findings on codependency, addiction, and dysfunctional behavior. By taking a good, honest look at our family life, perhaps we can break these cycles. By taking this time of life to look back on what we were taught as children and deciding whether or not these values and habits are important to us as adults of the 1990s, we can move out of perpetuating dysfunctional family/societal ways of learning and choose newer, healthier ways of living. This is "a time for searching, a time for losing."

My relationship with God was especially important. I couldn't have lived through this time of grieving for both husband and father if I had not trusted that God was caring for me. If we are honest with ourselves at the death of a parent, we admit that we are helpless and have no control over our lives. It is then we understand our need for the love, grace, and help of our creator. Prayer is our most important support during our grieving period. Chapter Five will discuss this in more detail.

Not only do we have to deal with our own grief, but if there is a surviving parent we need to help him or her through this difficult period. We also have to use this teachable moment to help our children understand and come to terms with death and the loss of a grandparent. It seems as if we are besieged from every direction. Many of us resonate to the phrase, "sandwich generation." We are caught in the middle between the elderly and the young. Chapters Six and Seven will give some hints to help us through this time.

Often we begin our grieving before a parent's death when we have to help with home care, hospital, or nursing home admittance. If our parent is suffering from Alzheimer's disease, heart problems, cancer, emphysema, or another debilitating illness, we need to make some difficult decisions. Chapter Eight presents some of the options before us when we are preparing for a parent's death.

In the final chapter I present some ideas to help us say goodbye to our loved ones. I encourage keeping alive the good memories of our parents by helping our children understand their heritage, and suggest ways that can help us grow and develop in our own lives.

We have to learn to deal with pain which arises from our life experiences way back into infancy and childhood. Arthur Schopenhauer put into words some of the feelings we may have when a loved one or close friend dies:

> The deep pain that is felt at the death of every friendly soul arises from the feeling that there is in every individual something which is inexpressible, peculiar to him alone, and is, therefore, absolutely and irretrievably lost ("Psychological Remarks" from *Parerga and Paralipomena*).

If we feel "deep pain at the death of every friendly soul," what are our feelings at the death of our father or mother? How do we measure pain? Is it pain we feel, or is our predominant emotion one of relief? anger? fear? guilt? loneliness? envy? longing for "the good old days"?

The death of a parent touches the very core of our being. The man or woman who nurtured us though childhood, protected us from harm, guided us through life's pitfalls, showed us how to cope with life, and finally allowed us to move out on our own had a profound influence—both good and bad—on our lives. Some of us had parents who prevented us from growing up, from moving out on our own; parents who ignored, abused, or neglected us. They did not prepare us for life's problems. Coming to terms with those memories requires what psychiatrist Elisabeth Kubler-Ross calls "grief work."

What is grief work? How do I deal with it? What are the emotional and physical symptoms of grief? How do I know if I need help? Where do I go for that help?

How do we learn to forgive? When we are grieving, we may experience both love and resentment. How can we be so mixed up? Sometimes we need to forgive our parents for their shortcomings, for their sins of omission as well as commission, for the times we were hurt both physically and emotionally.

If all the questions in this introduction make your head swim, don't let it discourage you. I hope to be able to explore ideas that will help you find answers. Each of us is a unique being, made by God with special qualities, experiences, and gifts. We relate to others in unique ways. No one can tell us: "This is the way to grieve for your parent." Each of us will grieve in our own way. By telling my story and those of others I hope to present new ideas that will help you move ahead with your own grief work.

We need to hear how other people have dealt with their problems and how new discoveries in the social sciences can help us in moving forward on our journey to God. We need to learn the difference between love, attachment, addictions and compulsions. We need to open the door and learn new ideas and fresh ways of looking at our lives. Hopefully these tools will be helpful when we again encounter pain and grief. They need to be used over and over as we continue our journey.

For me, it was important to learn about the teachings of the church. Not everything the ministers and pastors taught me was helpful, but the basic teachings, accumulated from the wisdom of the past two thousand years, helped me in my grief work.

Ecclesiastes says that there is "a time for tears, a time for laughter." It is my hope that you will be able to find your "time for laughter," to remember the good times and the bad, to close the door on this part of your life and move into the future.

One

Saying Goodbye

Grief drives men into habits of serious reflection,
sharpens the understanding
and softens the heart.

—*John Adams*

How do you say goodbye to a beloved parent? How do you say goodbye to the person

—whose patience taught you to communicate first with family and then with society?

—who physically protected you through your growing-up years and set down rules to help you survive an imperfect world?

—who encouraged you to try new things, develop new talents, explore your expanding world? And when you failed, was there to help you get up and try again?

How do you say goodbye to your mother

—who bore you in her womb, who nurtured, loved, fussed over you and finally—though sometimes with difficulty—let you leave and try your wings?

—who chauffeured you to ball games, track meets, music and swimming lessons?

—who taught you to cook, clean, run the washing machine and pick up your own mess, all of which contributed to the organization and stability of the family?

If you are her son, how do you say goodbye to the woman

—who taught you the meaning of love?

—who allowed you to be yourself even while you were learning that women indeed felt and thought differently than men?

If you are her daughter, how do you say goodbye to the woman

—who encouraged your femininity?

—who provided a shoulder to lean on?

—who acted as your role model, even when you swore you would never act like she did?

How do you say goodbye to your father

—who pointed out the wonders of nature?

—who passed to you his love of gardening?

—who read stories, loved, and comforted you?

—who attended baseball, football and basketball games night after night, season after season?

—who followed the track team from town to town and waited patiently for your turn to participate?

If you are his daughter, how do you say goodbye to the man

—who was your first love?

—who showed you how to live with and understand the masculine psyche?

—who had time to listen and give advice when you had a fight with your best friend?

If you are his son, how do you say goodbye to the man

—who was your role model?

—who loved and nurtured you?

—who patiently taught you how to "be a man" and, when the time came, sent you off into the world with his blessing?

How do you say goodbye to a parent who did none—or very little—of the above? How do you say goodbye to a parent

—who was a workaholic and spent very little time with you?

—who sexually abused you?

—who was an alcoholic and whose emotional extremes and mixed messages left you unable to trust?

—who physically abused you and your mother?

—who neglected or ignored you much of the time?

And in between both of those extremes, how do you say goodbye to parents

—who loved you but, because of their upbringing, had no idea how to express that love with words or hugs?

—who loved you but had unrealistic expectations for your future?

—who loved you but expected instant and complete obedience?

—who loved you but had no time to listen or never encouraged you to voice your hopes and dreams?

—who loved you but were so busy dealing with their own unresolved problems they never took time to look at yours?

—who loved you and did the very best they knew how at the time, but, because they were human, made mistakes?

How do we say goodbye to our parents? With difficulty! Grieving is hard work. Each of us grew up with a set of unique family rules and ideas which were enforced in varying degrees. Each of us has our own life story. Some families encouraged us, allowed us to take risks, praised and blessed us. Some families pushed, controlled, demanded conformity or ignored us. Some families gave us positive affirmation; some were negative. Most families gave us both.

How do we say goodbye to this parent who was a mixture of contradictions? There is no one way. There are no hard and fast rules. Each of us must come to terms with our feelings in our own way.

Growing Up with Our Parents

As an infant we were dependent on our parents for our every need. Without their love and care we would have died. Through their modeling we absorbed the "right" ways of acting, thinking, speaking and even feeling as we moved through childhood.

As children we gradually took on more responsibility for ourselves. We learned to stay away from hot stoves and the dangers of playing in the street. We learned to obey stop signs, to walk to school by ourselves and to get along with our peers. Slowly but surely our life experiences gave us the confidence and wisdom to move out on our own, and eventually to question our parent's rules and action.

Frequently we were confused when our parent told us to act one way, but behaved another. We all remember the sayings:

"Do as I say, not as I do."

"Don't air the family linen in public."

"We take care of our own."

"Don't let the neighbors know."

As adolescents we wanted to break away and experience life for ourselves, frequently causing heartbreak and conflict for both parent and child. Sometimes, with love and support from our parents, we managed to come through that difficult time; we learned to love and respect them as adults and friends. Others never learned to work through those ambivalent feelings and carried them into adulthood. Those unresolved feelings are often the basis of an uneasy truce between adult children and their parents.

If you are an abused child and have looked at your life from infancy to adulthood, you probably have become aware of feelings that you have ignored for many years. There is some difficult grief work ahead. If this violence was physical, verbal, emotional or sexual, your parent's death can bring many negative emotions to the surface.

Step by step all of us have to look over our past life, identify our emotions and decide how we personally are going to say goodbye. Many of us need help in going through these traumatic memories. I encourage you to find a therapist, counselor or a grief and growth group who will listen and support you during this grief work.

Identifying Emotions

As grief overwhelms us, many of the emotions we have felt, ignored or couldn't identify during our growing-up years will surface. What are these feelings that appear without our permission—almost spontaneously—at the time of death? Our first task is to identify, and label them. Only then can we decide if our way of coping is suitable for us as adults.

On the following list you will find some of the common feelings that most of us have when a parent dies. Because we each have our own life story, everyone will not relate to everything on the list. But we all will struggle with both the negative and the positive at one time or another during bereavement—from enormous relief to enormous loss, from anger and hate to love and thankfulness. We will feel confused and bewildered. We will wonder how to handle these feelings as we move through our daily routines.

Some Common Feelings We Experience

relief: "Now I am set free!"

apathy: "It doesn't affect me one way or another."

disbelief: "She can't be dead! I just talked to her on the telephone last night!"

love: "I loved my dad so much. How will I ever get along without him?"

hate: "He was cruel to me and my brothers and sisters. I hate him!"

mental and physical exhaustion: "I'm so tired and worn out that I can't get anything done or even think straight!"

guilt: "If only I had checked on her last night, maybe I could have saved her."

blame: "My sister didn't pay enough attention to mom. If she had gotten her to the doctor sooner, mom wouldn't have died."

anger: (at God) "Lord, you let mom die! I prayed so hard and you didn't answer my prayer!"

(at the church) "Our pastor didn't visit me at all after dad died. He didn't even try to comfort mom. I thought that was his business!"

(at the parent for dying) "How could you go and leave me just when you knew I needed you so much?"

(at the parent for his or her alcoholism) "I have lived with your drinking all my life, and I can't say I am sorry you are gone!"

(at a parent for past slights and emotional abuse) "You didn't pay any attention to my accomplishments when I was a child. You always loved my older sister more than you loved me!"

(at a parent for sexual and/or physical abuse) "I am so angry that I can hardly bear to think about the times you attacked me physically. You were sick!"

(at self for not preventing the death) "If I had shoveled that snow, then dad wouldn't have had his heart attack!"

(at a doctor, nurses or hospital) "The nurses didn't answer mom's call for help. She died because they weren't paying attention!"

confusion: "I came to the store for groceries, but now I can't remember what I needed. My mind just isn't functioning properly!"

bitterness: "Well, mom, you did it again! You always managed to throw a monkey wrench into everything I want to do! Now when I am leaving on my first vacation in three years, you stop me by dying!"

abandonment and orphanhood: "How could you leave me? Parents aren't supposed to leave their children!"

depression: "What's the use of living? The only person who ever understood and loved me has gone!"

loneliness: "I can't imagine coming into this house and not finding mom there! It won't be the same."

thankfulness: "I am so blessed to have had a father like that. Thank you, Lord."

loss of friendship: "When dad died I not only lost my father, I lost my best friend."

loss of humor: "I will miss my mom's sense of humor more than anything else. She could always find the funny side of anything that happened."

loss of a sounding board: "Where will I go for advice now? Dad was always willing to listen and point out ideas that I hadn't considered."

loss of T.L.C.:   "There will be a terrible void in my life now. Mom was always there when I didn't feel good or needed some tender loving care."

mixed feelings: "I am so mixed up! I know I should feel blue, depressed and have a sense of loss, but I don't at all! I'm relieved that dad's pain and suffering are over."

You can add other emotions to this list. Take time to write down those you are feeling right now. Keep your list and look at it later. Emotions change as you work through your grief.

Coping

Our feelings during mourning may be accompanied by actions that are out of the ordinary for us. Tears may turn up at inappropriate times and places—in the middle of the grocery store or when we attend church. We may go on a housecleaning binge, or spend hours working in the garden or fixing the car.

We may find ourselves unable to pray or attend church. It helps to know that all such responses are very normal; they don't signal we are losing our mind.

We can ease the pain, however. For example, I find that writing in my journal helps me through many restless days and nights. Just an ordinary spiral notebook kept by my bedside, where I can write down my feelings and emotions, my anger and depression help me shun those thoughts and relax my body.

When I don't feel like praying, taking ten to fifteen minutes for relaxation techniques helps me to let go of my worries and anxieties, and enables me to get back to work refreshed. Sometimes I take that time to tell God that I can't pray, or that I am very angry. Actually, telling God your feelings is praying. Conversation with God is as much a prayer as asking for help. The God who made us wants to hear exactly how we feel.

On the other hand, there are many actions we should recognize as warning signs: an inability to concentrate causing our work or studies to go downhill, excessive irritation and anger with family members, working overtime at the office or turning into a couch potato/TV watcher all day. Compulsive use of alcohol, drugs or gambling is also an indication that we are not dealing effectively with our grief. If you or a loved one are using these negative methods of coping, this may be a good time to look for professional help.

As a starter, you might ask yourself:

"I hurt! Do I want to continue this way?"

"What can I do to ease the pain?"

"Is this affecting my marriage?"

"What kind of an example am I giving my children?"

If compulsions and addictions have taken over, it is time to admit we can't recover alone. We need a surrogate family, people who are not emotionally involved with our family of origin and who will help us find new and more effective ways of reacting. Twelve-step groups—Alcoholics Anonymous (AA), Overeaters Anonymous (OA), Emotions Anonymous (EA) or Gamblers Anonymous (GA)—are waiting to help. Such groups provide reassurance and guidelines to get our lives under control. Finding a therapist or counselor who will provide individual guidance can be a literal lifesaver.

Perhaps this will be the hardest thing we ever do. Where do we find the strength to risk these new actions? Support from our loved ones and others is helpful, but basically this is a decision and a step we have to take on our own—with help from God. I have found that when I know what needs to be done but am blocked by fear, I have to pray: "Lord, give me the strength to take this step." or "Lord, take away my fear." It may take one week, one month, six months, a year or more, but eventually, in God's time, I will be able to take the risk. John Newton's eighteenth century folk hymn, *Amazing Grace*, says it all:

> Tis grace that brought me safe thus far,
> And grace will lead me home . . .

Identifying Our Masks

On Halloween, when ghosts and goblins rule the land, children don spooky masks and costumes to hide their identity. Adults do the same thing in everyday life as they try to disguise insecurities and low self-esteem or to conform to what they think others expect.

What do masks have to do with grief? They help keep the pain at bay. It is socially acceptable to show our grief when a parent dies. We receive much love, support and consolation at the time of the funeral and for a short while after. But before long our friends and co-workers want us to turn off the grief. They seem to say, "It's time to get on with your life!" Our grief, a reminder that death comes to all of us, makes them uncomfortable.

Or perhaps we are uncomfortable with some of our thoughts and feelings about our mother or father. We feel guilty when we dwell on the negative aspects of our relationship with our parents or things we should have done before they died. Perhaps we did not visit, phone or write very often in the last years; maybe we wish that we had said "I love you" before our parent died. All these feelings can be churning around inside us, but we do not allow the hurt or confusion to show. On the other hand, some of us put on a mask of intense grief because of some unfinished business or unresolved grudge that we had with our parent.

How many times has someone asked: "How are you getting along?" and you find yourself automatically responding:

"I'm getting along just fine," when really you want to say: "I hurt terribly and I don't think I will ever feel better!"

Or, "His death was a blessing; he was so sick," when you want to add: "but I am still devastated!"

Or, "I haven't got time to feel bad; I am too busy," when you know deep inside that you are running away from the pain. We are very adept at stuffing our guilty feelings behind our masks and refusing to look at them. Although inside we are vulnerable, lonely and fearful, outwardly we appear confident, cool and in control. Inside we may be searching for the love and comfort that we so desperately need, but outwardly we give the impression we need no one.

Often we ignore the feeling of worthlessness by comparing ourselves to others. Judgment calls on other people's actions are a form of masking our own. If we put them down far enough, then we look pretty good in comparison! Jesus told us to beware of this in his parable of the Pharisee and the tax collector, ". . . everyone who raises himself up will be humbled, but anyone who humbles himself will be raised up" (Lk 18:14).

The death of your parent is a good time to take a long, hard look at the masks you wear. Are those masks hiding a lot of hurt and pain which prevents you from being comfortable with yourself? Do they hide a lot of unresolved feelings left over from your childhood? Are you ready to say "I need to look at my growing-up years, try to understand what they have to do with the way I act today and resolve some of the unfinished business that I have with my parents?"

Looking the truth square in the face and becoming aware of the great love between parent and child, even while both made mistakes, are important steps in the healing process. This doesn't have to be a battle between ourselves and the truth; we don't have to beef up our will power and strike out with determination in our hearts. It is a matter of letting go and listening to the truth about ourselves and our parents. Ten to fifteen minutes a day of reflection is invaluable. God will speak to us if we just allow the time and space to hear his gentle whisper. We have only to open ourselves to receive the Word.

When you find the courage to take that step, "you will come to know the truth, and the truth will set you free" (Jn 8:32).

A Prayer Help

Dear Jesus,

I am really afraid tonight. I don't want to sit in quiet and solitude to hear the truth. I don't like myself all that well, and I'm scared to look deeply into the relationship with my parents. If I found the truth about me—about us—bad things could happen.

Maybe my heart would break!

Maybe I would find something so awful that I would be ashamed to face my family and friends!

Maybe the truth would inflict so much pain that I would carry it around for the rest of my life!

I'm scared!

Love, Cathleen

Dear Cathleen,

You and I have had many long talks, have spent much time together. Now I am asking you to take another big step.

I understand your fear.

I was afraid that night in Gethsemane and I asked my Father to take away the cup.

But when I said: "Your will be done," my Father gave me the peace and strength to follow his will.

I too will send you the grace to take this big step. Trust me. Remember that I love you.

Jesus

Two

Beginning the Healing

Pain slighted (is) pain remembered
—even if it (is) forgotten.

—Theron Raines

In this chapter I will offer some guidelines that have been helpful for me in dealing with grief. Perhaps they will provide some ideas that also will help you grow and develop.

Grief is a process, a continuing development involving many changes. We can't expect to move through this time in a hurry. The relationship with our mother or father grew and developed over a lifetime; it is unrealistic to expect to cut it off in a short period of time.

Perhaps the relationship with our parent declined rather than grew, regressed rather than developed. If that is so, we still need to look honestly and truthfully at ourselves and our parent. Perhaps now is the time we can choose to be our own person, let go of the guilt and anger we have felt for many years, and move in the direction that God is asking us to go.

Well-intentioned friends may tell us: "It has been six months since your mom died. That's long enough to grieve!" But there is no timetable for mourning. We work through feelings at our own pace. We can't let anyone try to hurry us. Grief work is hard work! To feel the pain and not try to stuff it inside requires courage. Some days we will have enough fortitude to take this on, and some days we won't. We need to acknowledge that we are human and that it will take some time to move along the road to acceptance.

If we try to repress our pain we will find that it has a way of popping up in very inopportune times and places. Frequently our family or work relationships are affected when we try to ignore our feelings. We may yell at our children or spouse, disagree with our coworkers, irritate our friends and generally foul up our lives. If we see this happening it is time to take a good look at ourselves. Perhaps one or two sessions with a therapist or counselor will help us sort out our feelings and start moving on the road to recovery.

It's OK to tell our loved ones and friends that we need time and space to work through our grief. It's all right to say "Have patience with me. I know that some days I am impossible to live with. I apologize if I have hurt your feelings." Or, "I need to be alone right now. But please ask again!" Being honest with yourself and others smooths the rocky path.

Grieving Time

Sometimes we just have to break down and cry. Sometimes we have to give vent to our anger. But we want to do that in an appropriate time and place.

Catherine, a single woman who had lived with her mother for many many years, told me that she would break into tears in the grocery store when she saw something that her mother particularly liked.

Jack and his father had golfed together for twenty years. He found that he couldn't watch the championship golf games on TV. He knew he would cry and "real men don't cry." After all, what kind of an example would that give his two boys? As time went on, he learned that showing tears in front of his children gave them permission to acknowledge their feelings about their grandpa's death. Tears were healing for both father and sons.

As strange as it sounds, I found that by scheduling periodic times for grieving I was not so apt to break down in front of other people. Many times I would get supper on the table, get the kids started eating, and then go upstairs to my bedroom and cry. By letting the tears flow I released the tension, let go of my need to control, and eventually ended up praying:

"Lord, I believe you will care for me and help me through this dark time. You are in charge of my life and I know that you will lead me in the right way."

Journaling

Keeping a journal can be a form of therapy. A cheap spiral notebook proved to be the beginning of my healing when I was grieving the deaths of my husband and my father. At first I just put down all my activities of the day, but gradually I began to write down my thoughts, feelings and prayers. I wrote about my anger, my loneliness, my sins, my joys, and my hurts and pains.

The waves of grief seemed to subside after I wrote my feelings down. The thoughts that circled endlessly in my head jumped onto the paper and stayed there. Because those notebooks were only for me to read, I learned to be more honest as I wrote, evaluating what I was doing with my life and setting goals for my future.

Don't edit what you write! Just write! If you don't know where to start—write these words: "I don't know where to begin," even if you have to write it five times before the words start to come. They will come!

I don't believe it is necessary to write each day. Sometimes days will go by between my entries, but when anxieties and worries start to pile up, I know it is time to get out my notebook. When I have a particularly good day I find myself writing about that also. I need to remember that my life consists of both good and bad days.

Learning to express myself in my journal was the beginning of my writing career. I wrote only for myself when I first began, but eventually I began writing reflections and opinions on political and church-related topics. I wrote letters to my children when they needed support or advice. Sometimes I wrote travelogues after I had taken a trip. I wrote to my representatives in Congress and other government leaders; I sent letters to the editor of area newspapers. Each time I wrote I found new courage to write more.

I am not saying this will happen to everyone. Each one of us has different talents and abilities. But writing in a journal can surely begin healing. It will make us aware of our own gifts and point out new opportunities in our lives. We do find the courage to move on.

Kindred Spirits

When I was a young girl *Anne of Green Gables* was my favorite book. I must have read it dozens of times. Anne had a special friend, Diana, a "kindred spirit" to whom she could tell her innermost thoughts without fear of rejection. A close friend, or group of friends, can be an important part of the healing process.

Not all of us have a friend we can confide in, but perhaps a pastor, minister or rabbi will be able to be a confidant. Counselors and therapists are trained to listen and point out new directions to consider. We are fortunate to live in a world where hospitals, hospices, churches and social service offices such as Catholic Family Services, Lutheran Social Services or the many non-denominational counseling services, provide grief and growth groups and individual therapists to help us through this difficult time. Local newspapers often run feature stories, ads and information about self-help groups. We can inquire in these different sources about meeting times and the costs involved.

Joining a group can be pretty scary if you have never done it before. Some people come and have no difficulty talking; others come and listen but do not join in the discussion. Most facilitators will assure you at the first meeting that you can listen, and then join in as much or as little as you want. Each person has different life experiences and is at a different point in the grief process. Contribute your insights to the extent that you are comfortable.

I recommend that you stay with the group for at least three meetings. Then if you feel you need to leave, at least you can say: "I gave it a good shot. That group is not for me." Finding a group or a therapist is like finding a doctor. With some you are comfortable, and others you are not. Don't be afraid to find another group if the relationship is not right.

Prayer

Just a word here about the importance of prayer. (Chapter Five covers this topic in more detail.)

First of all, don't be surprised if you can't pray. In the midst of our grief the last thing we seem to be able to do is talk to God. Prayer however, consists of much more than our usual requests for help.

Prayer is also telling our Creator exactly how we feel. We can inform God about all the anger, depression and frustration that we feel at the moment. If we want to scream out that God is a big bully who sends pain and suffering into the world, we can do so. If we want to yell and pound the table or a big pillow, that's OK. God is big enough to handle that. As Christians, we believe that God became human—Jesus. God understands how hard it is to be human, how difficult it is to accept pain and suffering. We should never forget that, even with all our anger, God loves us and waits for us to express our feelings and finally to say, "Lord, help me!"

Journaling can help us here. Write a letter to God telling him about all your feelings. That too, is prayer. It's consoling to write out a dialogue with Jesus. For example:

Cathleen: "I am so angry about dad's death that I can't think straight. It is all your fault, God. You have failed me!"

You might find Jesus writing back to you through your pen or pencil:

Jesus: "I understand that anger, Cathleen. You feel helpless and out of control. I felt that way as I prayed in the garden at Gethsemane. I had to let go of my plans and do my Father's will."

Sometimes Jesus' answers or insights are a surprise. We really don't know what will come up on the paper. If nothing comes when we make a sincere attempt to dialogue, don't worry about it. The time is obviously not right. Put away the paper and try again in a few days. Patience is a good virtue to cultivate when working through grief.

Taking Care of Your Body

Grief can cause a drain on the emotions, your body and your ability to concentrate. We feel exhausted and unable to get any work done. Grief can also do just the opposite. We can be filled with nervous energy and fill our lives with one job after another, taking on more than we can handle. We need to strive for a happy medium. Treating ourselves with tender, loving care is probably the most important thing we can do right now. TLC means being aware of our needs and making sure that we answer those needs to the best of our ability.

Scheduling time for rest and relaxation should be on the top of the list if we tend to overwork in order to discount our feelings. We should go to that movie we have been wanting to see; take the family on a special outing—a picnic, miniature golf, bowling, a visit to a nearby lake to enjoy the quiet; read a good book; attend a concert. I have found that a three-day visit to a nearby monastery gives me time to enjoy the solitude and silence, focus on myself and come back to my daily routine refreshed and rejuvenated.

Those of us who tend to withdraw from daily activity when grieving, need to make an effort to reach out and do something that takes us out of our shells. Even if it is only one small step a day, that effort will help us out of the deep, black pit and make the next step that much easier.

Sometimes it is difficult to decide just which way to go. If so, therapy or counseling will help us sort out our options.

Sufficient sleep at night is also very important, although sometimes quite difficult. I found myself waking up in the middle of the night unable to sleep, mentally taking care of all the jobs I had lined up for the next day. I finally learned to relax my whole body as I crawled into bed each night, taking each job, chore, and worry and putting it safely inside an imaginary black velvet bag. When I got all of them in, I pulled the drawstrings shut and put it under the bed. Then my last prayer of the night was:

> Lord, I give you this bag full of worries. I am sure you are capable of taking care of the world without me—at least for tonight. If I need them in the morning I will ask for them back, but in the meantime, they are your responsibility.

A smile and a sense of humor can be relaxing.

Exercise

It seems that every magazine on the newsstands tell us how important it is to have a certain amount of physical activity in our lives. That is no less true for the grieving person. Scientists have found that exercise stimulates the production of the hormone endorphin in our brain which in turn reduces depression.

We have a variety of exercise choices: running, jogging, bicycling, golfing, aerobics, swimming, bowling, tennis—the list goes on and on. Many people find that a brisk walk three or four times a week gives them a new lease on life. The Red Cross promotes water-walking as an excellent exercise many non-swimmers enjoy.

Diet and Nutrition

It is very easy to rely on fast foods, quick pickup meals and TV dinners when we are experiencing grief, even when we know that a steady diet of these foods is not good nutrition. For optimum health we need the right amount of carbohydrates, proteins, fat, fiber, vitamins and minerals. They provide the necessary nutrients for mental and physical health.

How do we decide what foods will give us this good nutrition when we are bombarded daily by magazines, newspapers and television ads telling us to eat an advertised product? Each one claims to be the best. They tell us that "no-cholesterol" margarine or "fat free" salad dressing is the only kind to keep us healthy. That fiber cereal with fruit added not only will keep us going all morning, but also reduce the risk of cancer! How can we decide what is right?

Nutritionists, including the U.S. Department of Agriculture, the National Cancer Institute and the National Food Processors Association, recommend a balanced diet based on a four-level pyramid.

Grains are found at the base of the pyramid. These include bread, rice, pasta, and cereals of which we should eat six to eleven servings a day (what constitutes a serving varies from food to food).

Fruits and vegetables are found on the next level. We should eat three to five servings of vegetables and two to four servings of fruit each day.

The third level shows dairy products, meat, poultry, fish, beans, eggs and nuts. Two to three servings a day are recommended. Fats, oils and sweets are found at the top of the pyramid and should be used sparingly.

This graphic way of showing the different requirements from each food group helps us make sense out of the confusing advertising information. To provide expert advice, the American Dietetic Association maintains a national hot line (800-366-1655) which can be called between 10AM and 5PM, eastern standard time, Monday through Friday.

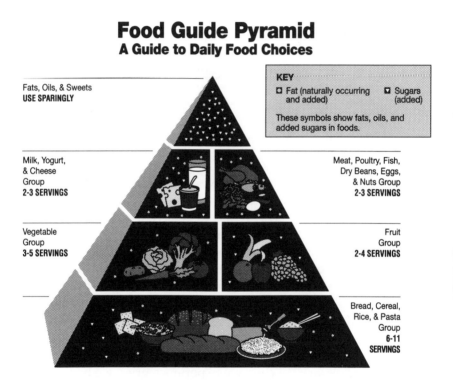

Food Guide Pyramid
A Guide to Daily Food Choices

Fats, Oils, & Sweets
USE SPARINGLY

KEY
◻ Fat (naturally occurring and added) ◪ Sugars (added)

These symbols show fats, oils, and added sugars in foods.

Milk, Yogurt, & Cheese Group
2-3 SERVINGS

Meat, Poultry, Fish, Dry Beans, Eggs, & Nuts Group
2-3 SERVINGS

Vegetable Group
3-5 SERVINGS

Fruit Group
2-4 SERVINGS

Bread, Cereal, Rice, & Pasta Group
6-11 SERVINGS

U.S. Department of Agriculture
Human Nutrition Information Service

39

Some of us use food to ease our emotional pain. We may eat the "comfort foods" that made us feel better when we were younger. This childhood memory is a form of denial, a tried and true way of coping with our changing life. When I was a little girl, my mother and my aunts who lived next door would give me homemade bread with butter and brown sugar for a special treat. Frequently my solution for emotional upsets is to have a sweet roll, several cookies or a bowl of ice cream—poor nutrition as well as an inappropriate way of suppressing my feelings.

On the other hand some of us find food repulsive during grieving, and don't want to eat at all. This is also destructive, not only because we do not get the proper nutrients, but because this reinforces false ideas about our dealing with pain. (In Chapter Four I will address these childhood ways of coping as the basis for an addiction.)

Addictions

If we watch television, we know that we have our choice of innumerable brands of pain relievers for every imaginable illness. We are led to believe that all we need is one little pill to help us sleep, or perhaps two or three little pills to get rid of every bodily ache and pain. If stress is upsetting our life, there is also a pill for that. The advertising industry has a vested interested in telling us that life can be pain free—but of course only if we use a certain brand of drug!

I suggest that we take a good look at the substances we take each week or month and ask ourselves, "Is all this really necessary?" When we experience grief, we have to go through pain at one time or another. It can be postponed, but without a doubt it will erupt in very unexpected times and places. Perhaps now is the time to say: "No more pills!" It will not be easy, but there are many places we can go for help. The slogan "Just Say No" is catchy to hear, but it takes much more than a few words if we are serious about stopping. A twelve-step program can give practical, down-to-earth help to those trying to get through the day without the crutch of pills and drugs.

I found out the hard way that an excess of caffeine was making me restless and unable to sleep at night, and jumpy and irritable during the day. When I became aware that caffeine is an ingredient in many food products such as chocolate, baked goods, frozen dairy products, gelatins, puddings, soft candies and colas, and not just coffee, I was able to cut down my intake of that drug and get a good night's sleep. This experience taught me to read the labels on food and medicines so I would know what I was eating.

Social service and counseling groups can help us as the healing begins. Take a look in your newspaper or the yellow pages of the phone book for local groups' meeting times and places. I have also included names and addresses of different helps in the bibliography.

Some of the most helpful advice I received came from reading books. Every bookstore has many inexpensive self-help paperbacks which give us insights into ourselves and our behavior. Some are also listed in the bibliography.

These resources and beginning ideas are meant to help you as you start through the grieving process. Most of them are just here to trigger your own ideas in helping yourself. Only you can know what applies and what doesn't. Be honest with yourself. Hiding your grief and worries can only cause problems later on. Above all, don't be afraid to ask for help. God made us social beings. At some time in our lives we need advice, comfort, and love from others. Reach out for that help one step at a time.

A Prayer Help

Dear Lord,

Sometimes there is so much confusion and so many decisions to make that I can't imagine how I will ever handle the next day, let alone the next month or year.

I remember that when you were overwhelmed you stopped what you were doing and spent time in prayer.

Help me to take a few minutes each day to talk and listen to you. After all, there is nothing that you and I together can't handle.

Amen.

Three

Grief and Mourning

"Grief for a while was blind . . ."

—Percy Shelley

Although Shelley wrote in the early nineteenth century, he surely understood the nature of beginning grief. It wasn't until the 1970s however, that Elisabeth Kubler-Ross, a Swiss psychiatrist, published her pioneer work *On Death and Dying*, listing stages common to people who are dying: denial, anger, bargaining, depression and acceptance. Later research showed that the families and loved ones of the dying also go through this series of roller coaster feelings. Since then, Dr. Kubler-Ross has written other books on death, dying, and grief, teaching us to deal with our inner turmoil when we lose someone we love.

Learning more about her work can help us identify our particular level of grief and find out what we can do about it.

Denial

At first we don't want to see what is actually happening; we close our eyes to reality because it is too painful. We say things like:

The doctor can't possibly be right when he says that mom has only six months to a year to live. Let's look for another doctor!

43

My dad is only fifty-two years old. He can't have cancer; he doesn't even smoke!

Mom looks great and has all kinds of energy. The doctors don't know what they are talking about!

Dad can't be dead in a car wreck! He and mom were leaving tomorrow to come and visit us!

This is a very necessary defense when we first learn of our loss (or impending loss). Our bodies, minds and emotions are unable to absorb all the bad news at once; we take in only as much as we can handle at the moment.

When someone in the family shows signs of denial, don't try to talk them out of it. When they are ready to acknowledge the bad news, they will do so. Working through the stages of grief is hard work, and people do that only at their own time and pace. We can help by allowing those who are grieving to express their feelings and being there for them when they become aware of the pain.

Anger

Anger is many things: a powerful emotion, a stage of grief, an incentive for working constructively through a problem, or a reason for lashing out at the world and the people around us. A capacity for anger is with us from birth. Some psychologists say a baby can feel anger while still in the womb. It is true that some people show their anger more than others, but everyone—absolutely everyone—feels anger.

So here we are, trying to come to terms with the death or approaching death of our parent and one of the emotions we feel is a burning rage. How do we handle feelings like:

If mom had not smoked so much she wouldn't have died of cancer!

44

Dad was a workaholic! Not only did he not have any time for his children while we were growing up, but he deprived my children of a grandfather because his overwork brought on a heart attack!

Mom has had diabetes for fifteen years. If she had taken better care of herself she wouldn't be dead now!

Dad drank himself to death. Not only that, he made my life a living hell while he was alive! I can't say that I am sorry he is gone!

We just found out that mom has Alzheimer's disease. How could dad die and leave me all alone to handle these next years?

There are as many ways to express anger as there are people, and many of us do not express it in a healthy manner. For example: perhaps we were taught as children that it was wrong to express anger, so we learned to push our feelings down inside. We swallowed them and, consciously or unconsciously, learned not to look at them. Such an unhealthy response can lead to a later explosion when we can no longer keep those feelings suppressed.

Perhaps we have a lot of unexpressed feelings about our parents, some buried quite deep, some just below the surface. Over time the anger festers before the lid finally blows off.

Perhaps a parent subjected us to verbal, emotional, sexual or physical abuse when we were children and this anger is now being expressed destructively about another topic, or with another person. It may be that we are not aware that the abuse and anger we direct at someone close to us can be a sign that we need to look into ourselves and say "Why?"

When I find myself overwhelmed by anger, I ask these questions: "Do I have the right to be angry about this? Is my anger legitimate? Am I angry about something else and just now find it coming out in a different direction?"

Only after exploring the answers to these questions can I ask myself "What do I choose to do about it?" This gives me some time to cool down and think rationally before I jump all over the person who happens to be handy at the moment. This way of dealing with anger is something I am still working on, but I am learning.

We might also ask ourselves if we need to consult a therapist or counselor who will help us through the problem.

Perhaps we are so angry that we have to physically get rid of the rage we are feeling. Dr. Kubler-Ross holds periodic workshops where she encourages grieving people to pound on a mattress to rid themselves of the suppressed anger that no longer can be contained. If our anger is that intense, these remedies should be done only with the help and support of a therapist.

What we do with our anger can be positive or negative. If we scream, yell, strike out at those around us or transfer our anger to another person or relationship, we are choosing a destructive, negative way of dealing with our feelings. If we count to the proverbial ten, recognize the anger for what it is, and try to identify the cause, we will be well on our way to a healthy response to the erupting emotion.

After recognizing the feeling and identifying the cause, we must decide whether or not we want to communicate this to the person we perceive to be the cause or object of our anger. If we decide to do so, it is important to articulate this positively, not negatively. John Power, C.P. says that "anger is not a weapon to be used for destruction, but a feeling to be shared for greater mutual understanding." There are appropriate and inappropriate ways of doing this.

Think about how you are going to tell this person that you are angry. Try using the "I" statements instead of the accusing "you." Instead of saying:

Doctor, *you* made me angry when you walked out of the room instead of talking to my mother the other day!

try:

I am feeling angry right now because I felt deserted when you didn't take the time to talk to my anxious mother about my dad's illness!

or

I can see that my sick mother was upset and confused when you talked only to me and the nurses in the room. Would you please make it a point to speak directly to her since she is perfectly able to understand what you are saying.

Using the "I" sentences which express personal emotions such as "I feel," "I am aware," or "I can see" diffuses an angry reply. The accusatory "you" encourages an angry response. Dialogue is much more apt to follow if we don't verbally point a finger at another.

Often, in order to do this, I have to step back, almost literally walk away from the person and give myself time to adjust to a new way of dealing with anger. It is during this time that I pray for the insight and courage to see this through, that I will use love and not revenge as a basis for my confrontation.

Anger at God is a very common reaction when we are grieving for a parent. After all, God could have spared our mom or dad all that suffering and pain, right?

How can God make a good person like my dad suffer so much?

Why should my mom have to lay in bed, a victim
of Alzheimer's disease for seven years?

We ask ourself why? why? why? over and over again
and never receive an answer that satisfies us.

Rabbi Harold Kushner, in *When Bad Things Happen to
Good People*, says that we are asking the wrong question
when we ask "why?" He says that the correct question is:
"What can I learn from this pain and hurt in my life?"
Reflecting on this has been very helpful in dealing with
my anger. I can't change what is happening, but I can
change my outlook.

Expressing our outrage to God is all right. God is
strong enough to handle that anger without lashing back
as we might do. Our faith teaches us that our creator loves
us and would never do anything to hurt us, even when we
are angry.

Telling the source of our being everything that is
going on in our life, including our feelings, hurts, and
pains, is the first step in dialoguing with God—in other
words, prayer. Dialogue requires two people however, so
we have to make time to listen to God's response as well
as share our deepest feelings. If we are caught up in how
to solve our problems by ourselves, we can hardly hear
what the Lord is trying to say to us. Listening for a
response to our prayer allows us to discern God's will,
even if it requires much patience on our part to be quiet
enough to listen. Chapter Five gives a few more ideas on
prayer as a dialogue with God.

Bargaining

Bargaining is a stage that some of us go through, and
others seem to ignore completely. Those who are helping
a parent through a long, painful illness are more apt to find
themselves bargaining—sometimes with the doctors, but
more often with God. Some people find themselves thinking things like:

If you will just let mom live until her last child graduates from school, I will go to Mass every morning without fail.

If dad can live until my brother's wedding is over, then I won't ask for anything more.

Please let dad attend his grandson's graduation next month. I will give extra time at the soup kitchen for the next year!

This bargaining can apply to confirmations, weddings, baptisms, birth of the next grandchild—almost any big occasion we look forward to. Or it can be more general:

Let mom get over this cancer and I will be more kind, caring and gentle in all my relationships!

We try to enter into an agreement with God that will postpone the inevitable. It sometimes looks shortsighted to those of us who are on the outside of the grieving process, and to a certain extent it is. But for others it is a necessary part in gradually dealing with our loss. We need to have patience with ourselves and others when going through this process.

Depression

Anger and rage often lead to another stage, depression. This may be accompanied by guilt and anger with ourselves. In fact, depression is defined as anger turned inward against oneself. When we are depressed we feel helpless, floundering, low and lifeless. We can have feelings of self-pity, self-hatred, guilt, fear, sadness, loneliness and indifference. It is reflected in feelings like:

I don't feel like getting out of bed this morning. I haven't got any energy at all.

I'm so very, very lonesome since mom died. She and I were good friends and now I have no one to be my sounding board. I am just going to lie here on the couch and fall asleep, then I won't have to think about it.

I don't want to go anyplace or do anything since my folks died. I took care of them for so many years and now I have nothing to look forward to.

Sometimes we are lethargic when depressed. Other times we respond by doing the opposite. We rush from activity to activity, take on more than we can handle and then drop exhausted into bed—all so we won't have to deal with the feelings that keep surfacing when we are quiet.

Depression was an aggravating step for my family and friends. My emotions were out-of-control; tears flowed at inopportune times and places. I blamed myself, not for my father's death, but for the fact that I hadn't gone to visit him very often the year before he died. The fact that he lived eighteen hundred miles away while I was trying to get my life straightened out after the death of my husband the year before, didn't excuse me from my feelings of guilt. I should have handled it all perfectly!

It is easy to be on the outside of a situation and see what can be done and what is impossible. But when we are grieving, we are very much a part of the situation. We don't think rationally or logically. In my case I was letting my emotions rule my life.

To regain my balance I had to look at realistic and unrealistic guilt. It is important to understand the difference and identify which kind is causing your depression. Unrealistic guilt says:

I should have done more for my parents; they should have come first in my life no matter how many other obligations I had.

Realistic guilt says:

I have injured my mother/father by what I have done (or not done), but I did the very best I could with the time and energy that I had.

That kind of guilt has a basis in reality.

You might say:

I should have checked on mom more often. Then she wouldn't have lain alone on the kitchen floor for so long before anyone found her.

Of course, we have our own family to get to school and a full time job besides! We couldn't be with mom every minute. We need to answer the question: "Is this guilt realistic, or are we requiring an impossible perfection?"

Sometimes we have to acknowledge that we did not make an effort to help a parent when needed and could have easily made the time to do so. Perhaps we ignored warning signs that should have indicated that a parent was ill. This might be a realistic guilt.

As we reflect on our guilt we need to beware of the "shoulds" and "oughts."

I should have spent more time with my folks.

I ought to have insisted that dad go to the doctor.

I should have seen that dad had his license taken away. He had no business driving a car.

If we find that our guilt is realistic, the next step is to ask for forgiveness from the parent, from God and from ourselves. Sometimes that last one is the most difficult.

Some people find forgiveness by visiting a parent's grave and apologizing for their mistakes or neglect. Others find it helpful to write a letter to their dead parent, asking forgiveness for their actions. Or they visit with a minister or priest who can help them see God's loving forgiveness. Catholics can also find forgiveness through the rite of reconciliation.

If depression starts to affect our daily life and relationships, then it is time to see a therapist or counselor. None of us can go through life without the help of others. Since God made us social beings, we need to rely on each other, even when it is difficult to ask for help.

Acceptance

There is a difference between acceptance and resignation. Resignation is a sterile attitude in which the death is seen as a surrender to the inevitable: "God is all-powerful, and I can't do anything about it." Acceptance is the goal we all strive for, and sometimes it seems very elusive. It is a time when, having grieved through the earlier stages, we accept the reality of our loss. It is a time when we experience a peace and calmness that allows us to look ahead and get on with our life—a time of a new beginning. In acceptance, we acknowledge that God, loving us unconditionally, will help us deal with the hurts and pains of this world and show us the way to grow from our experiences.

These stages of grief do not come in any special intensity or order. In fact, some experts prefer not to use the terminology "stages of grief." They believe it implies we move logically and orderly from one step to another. This does not happen. Most of us jump from one to another, backward and forward, from anger to depression and sometimes back to denial. We may experience little denial, much anger, some depression and then move on to acceptance without any bargaining period at all. We may not even experience any anger. That's OK. These stages are not rigid; each person's experience is unique. But the stages summarize feelings that research has shown most people experience sometime during their grief.

For me, my experience of the stages helped to validate my feelings—to know that I was not weird, losing my mind, or "sinning" because of my feelings. Reading Kubler-Ross's books helped me be aware that I could work through those feelings and emerge on the other side of grief.

Grief is a feeling of intense anguish at the time of bereavement, loss or failure. Is there anything we can do to help ourselves through this difficult time? When my father died twenty years ago, not too many places offered help. Today there are many grief and growth support groups that are a safe place to vent your feelings and help you move ahead. (See bibliography for information.)

Above all, we need to remember to be kind and gentle with ourselves. We can't work it out on a timetable. Each of us is a unique, special human being with different life experiences. Turning ourselves over to God and trusting that the source of all being will lead us through this difficult time can help us find the patience to work through the pain and hurt.

A Prayer Help

Dear Lord,

Sometimes I feel like I am a bouncing rubber ball—hitting denial, bargaining and anger, then back to denial and immediately into depression.

Add my guilt to that because I wasn't perfect and my head just whirls. Will I ever come to rest?

Please, Lord, remind me to take a few minutes each morning to sit in your presence and feel your love. The bouncing rubber ball just wants to sit and rest with your loving hand on me.

Amen.

Four

Breaking
the Cycle

Family secrets act as the plaque
in the arteries of communications.

—*Edwin Friedman*

Once upon a time there was a little village where
the people had a special ceremony every summer
solstice. They would line up in the village square
at sunrise, all the parents on the north and all the
children on the south. Each mother or father would
walk across the square and formally present a
special package to the child. Sometimes the
parents would present two or three, but each year
they would give at least one.

To one little girl, the mother might give the virtue
of honesty and truthfulness, the father the trait of
frugality. A little boy might receive the gift of
laughter from his father, but a "gift" of compulsive
overeating from his mother. Another little boy
might find courtesy and helpfulness in the package from his mother, but a gambling addiction
from his father. Sometimes a child would receive
the gift of alcoholism from her mother, but a great
love of people from her father.

Someone else would receive sexual addiction from one parent and an ability to be well organized from the other. A little boy down the line would open his hands to find fear and shyness. Right next to him a little girl might receive a love of education and learning, but also a great fear of taking risks. Perfectionism, excessive control, love of people, an ability to make friends, fiery tempers, workaholism—there was no end to the positive and negative gifts that parents presented to their children.

Most of the time the parents were completely unaware that they were presenting negative gifts. Because they had received them from their own parents, they automatically handed them down to their children.

Each year the children grew and developed. By the time they were young adults, ready to leave home, some realized that they wanted to decline one or more of the gifts they had received as children. They attended yet another ceremony in the village square. This time their parents were not present. Instead, on the opposite side stood a row of other adults. Each one wore a sign designating a helping profession: Alcoholics Anonymous (AA), clinical psychologist, sexual addiction counselor, minister, rabbi, priest, social services, counselor, Emotions Anonymous (EA), Gamblers Anonymous (GA), Lutheran Social Services counselor, Catholic Family Services, campus minister, no-smoking adviser, listening friend, mental health therapist, and many others.

Each young person attended this ceremony because he or she had decided to decline a parental gift. For some, letting go of the gift would be relatively easy; for others, gifts had become firmly attached over the years. A person could not just drop the gift on the ground and leave it there in the square.

If, however, the person handed the gift to a helper on the other side, the helper could support and assist the person in finding a way to let go of the unwanted gift. It might take only a listening moment and friendly support. It might take years of therapy. And the counselor could assist in detaching the person from other unwanted gifts, or direct the person to another counselor if necessary.

Of course, not all the young adults realized the need for this special ceremony. Some got married, had families, and handed on the compulsions and addictions they had received from their parents to a new generation, unaware that they were doing so. Some attended the ceremony in their middle years, others when they were older. Some never attended. But the village always welcomed men and women, at any age, to join in the rite of passage that they needed to become self-actualized adults.

Dealing with Negative Gifts

Just like the children in the fable, we have been given both positive and negative gifts from our parents. Do we have to accept them and even pass them on? If we have already given those traits and habits to our children, is it too late to change? Absolutely not.

For that matter, the death of a parent can provide a kind of "teachable moment," an opportunity to become aware of and assess our actions, decline the negative gifts and choose a new way. Death and the ensuing grief can be the catalyst that inspires a review of our lives and encourages us to make changes that will shape future relationships.

This is a big and difficult undertaking. To begin with we need to understand some of the categories of negative gifts. In recent years counselors, therapists, ministers, and other helping professionals have tried to show us ways to break harmful generational cycles while showing us new ways of relating to each other. In so doing they have introduced a whole new vocabulary. It is useful to understand some of these terms, so let's take a short look at three of them. If you want to learn more about a particular subject, there is a list of recommended books and tapes at the end of the book.

Twenty years ago addiction meant simply "giving oneself up to a strong habit," the word "codependency" didn't even appear in the dictionary and dysfunctional wasn't used in relation to individuals or social systems. What do they mean today?

Addiction

Writing in *When Society Becomes an Addict*, Anne Wilson Schaef defines addiction as "any process over which we are powerless. It takes control of us, causing us to do and think things that are inconsistent with our personal values and leading us to become progressively more compulsive and obsessive."

Gerald May, a well-known psychiatrist, author and spiritual director, defines addiction in his book *Addiction and Grace* as "compulsive habitual behaviors that eclipse our concern for God and compromise our freedom." When we are addicted to a certain substance or action, we are giving up the freedom to choose the parameters of our actions. We are letting those actions be determined by the addiction—not by our free choice.

So we need to expand the limits of addiction to an understanding more inclusive than compulsive drinking, eating, gambling, or sex. For example, we can also be addicted to such behaviors as perfectionism, power, work, even the control and manipulation of others. The list is almost endless.

Some experts claim that 96 percent of the population has an addiction of one kind or another. I recently went through May's list of addictions and found at least twelve I recognized personally—and my family could probably identify a few more!

In addition, we move from one addiction to another. Recovering alcoholics frequently find themselves with an insatiable desire for sweets—card shops now have whole sections devoted to those who label themselves "chocoholics." Ex-smokers tend to put on weight because they eat more after giving up the nicotine. Perhaps our whole life is a story of letting go of our addictions, one after another, in order to find God.

Not only do these addictions affect family relationships, but they can affect our relationship with our Creator. The first commandment, "for you will worship no other god . . ." (Ex 34:14) does not just refer to the pagan gods of Moses' era. Anytime we make an object or idea more important than our Creator, we are making that our god, turning away from God's life-giving love. The addiction becomes our God.

Codependence

Melody Beattie, in her ground-breaking work *Codependent No More* defines codependence as "a condition in which a person has let someone else's behavior affect him/her, or is obsessed with controlling other people's behavior."

I like the definition Fr. Peter McCall, OFM Cap, uses in *The Healing of Codependence* where he succinctly describes it "a psychological need to be needed." A good example is the wife of an alcoholic husband. She enables him to keep on drinking—even though she disapproves—by putting him to bed when he comes home drunk, cleaning up after him when he is sick or making excuses to his employer when he can't go to work. She is actually making it easier for him to continue in his addiction while meeting her emotional needs by becoming a "rescuer." She's the "heroine," the "responsible wife," the "dependable" member of the family. But inside she is just as sick as he. She is codependent.

Codependency occurs in many areas of our lives. All of us, at some time or another, think we need other people to depend on us in some way as a means of coping with our feelings of loneliness, helplessness and pain. That is just part of being human. If, however, we become overly dependent on others to assure us of our self-worth, to show us the love that we can never seem to find, or to rescue us when we are in trouble, then we are codependent. In reacting to life's problems and pains, rather than acting to change our responses, we build up habits that get progressively worse.

Dysfunctional

Dysfunctional is another word we hear with increasing frequency. It means that an impairment exists, that something is not functioning the way it should. In family life, the label dysfunctional means the family does not answer its own needs. For example if the father is an alcoholic and the mother enables his alcoholism and becomes codependent in caring for him, we would say that the children grow up in a dysfunctional family. Often they acquire serious problems of their own as a result of the family dynamic. Perhaps one child tries to keep peace by making excuses and trying to please the parents; another child might simply rebel and behave in a delinquent manner.

Family Secrets, Rules, and Silences

Another source of negative gifts are family secrets, rules, and silences. All families have topics we were not allowed to discuss as children and which may have stayed with us as we formed our own immediate families. This "silence in the family" was used to hide unacceptable conduct or to ignore subjects that were embarrassing, frightening, or not fully understood. Families did not talk about the developmentally disabled, a relative's arrest, homosexuality, alcoholism, gambling, or drug addiction. Sex, including menstruation, physical and emotional changes at puberty, pregnancy and intercourse were subjects that were never mentioned in polite company. At the top of the "silence" list were rape, incest, and abuse, be it physical, sexual, emotional or verbal.

Keeping family secrets or refusing to talk about certain topics constructs psychological roadblocks which prevent communication between parent and child. This in turn contributes to an unending cycle of negative gifts passing from one generation to another. Rabbi Edwin Friedman, D.D., author and family therapist, says: "Secrets allow the demons an opening into the next generation. . . . Events in a family can have lingering effects for four generations."

Silence in the family leads to unwritten family rules which reinforce the keeping of secrets.

"Don't let the neighbors know!"

"Don't air your dirty linen in public!"

"We take care of our own!"

Just before my paternal aunt died at age ninety-three, she confided that my grandparents had run away to a different state and were married by a judge. Neither my sisters nor my mother ever knew this and though it brought a smile to our faces now, we knew it could never have been mentioned when I was growing up. Marrying outside the faith brought shame on the family.

There are many such realities that are still very difficult to acknowledge—for example, an alcoholic parent even though Alcoholics Anonymous has helped us understand and discuss the topic more openly. When a gay or a lesbian decides to "come out of the closet," family relationships can be turned upside down. Accusations of child and spousal abuse cause turmoil not only in families, but in society as a whole.

Recently my sisters and I spent several afternoons reminiscing and talking about our childhood. As the oldest child I remembered entirely different incidents than my two younger sisters. Their experiences with my parents, grandparents, aunts and uncles were not part of my life but provided helpful insights into family behavior patterns.

My childhood memories include a time during the 1930s when my father and uncle decided to make beer in our basement. I was old enough to realize that we weren't to tell anyone about it, but my younger sister had no such scruples. She used the story for "show and tell" in her first-grade class. Several of her classmates repeated her tale at home, and my parents had a rash of calls saying: "I'll be right over" or "save me some!" Some "secrets" become part of the family's trove of humor.

Getting the Family Picture

In any era the function of the family is to answer our needs. In the past these were nearly always solely focused on economic and educational functions. In today's fast-paced, high-tech, high-stress world, family function can be summed up with one word—relational. Our needs now are for better communication between family members as we try to balance work, homelife and recreation; and for a love that nourishes this open communication and growth.

To understand if these categories are at work in our own families, it's helpful to get an overall family picture. It can help us identify our gifts, both positive and negative.

One way to start is to visit aunts, uncles, cousins, parents, old family friends, or neighbors. Try to get them to talk and reminisce about the old times. They'll often recall surprising stories and incidents, such as the information that one of your uncles ran away from home and stayed away for five years. Try to find out the reason behind such an action. It might shed some light on topics that were never discussed within the family.

Another example is that of an acquaintance. His mother had been very negative about his decision to marry. He expected it though, because she also made it very difficult for his older brothers. Imagine how perplexed he was when he found out decades later that this very same mom had eloped herself because her mother had stood in the way of her marriage. He's decided this behavior won't make it to a third generation.

Dates of death or divorce can be found in courthouse records. Checking cemeteries where you know your forebears were buried often reveals that one or more children died in infancy. Did this death contribute to a divorce in the family several years later? That does happen.

Perhaps you have to clean out the old family home after a parent's death. Keep an eye open for old newspaper clippings, diaries, or journals. They are an invaluable source of family history.

At reunions or get-togethers, an aunt or uncle might mention Great-Uncle John's alcoholism or Aunt Helen's pregnancy before marriage. Perhaps we hear about a baby who died at birth or during childhood from the dreaded diphtheria, whooping cough, or in a flu epidemic. Sometimes during a final illness we hear our mother or father mention the death of a sibling, and how they had not been allowed to talk about it as they grew up. Our unknown family stories can help us form a picture of our family of origin.

You might find it helpful to construct a genogram, or family diagram. Harriet Goldhor Lerner offers a detailed and graphic explanation of how to do a genogram in *The Dance of Intimacy*. She defines it as a pictorial representation of the facts of a family system for at least three generations. Charting a diagram which includes the family's names, ages, and dates of change will give you an overall picture of how deaths, divorces, traumatic events, and behavior patterns have affected your whole family.

The strengths, weaknesses, and dysfunctional areas of your family will become evident as you work on this chart.

Stop for a minute and see if you can recall some of the rules which were part of your childhood, perhaps carried down from many previous generations. Don't be surprised if your children have learned them, even if you have never explicitly said, "This is a family rule!" By formulating unspoken and unwritten rules, families avoid the discussion of painful topics and hope that ignoring them will make them go away. These secrets do not disappear. On the contrary, they contribute to a lack of communication and put up barriers between family members.

One unwritten rule which perpetuated silence in my family of origin was "Don't question the rules!" I believe that the death of a parent can be a serendipitous moment in our lives, one which challenges us to break that rule. If we have been following our parent's value system without using God's gift of free will to choose for ourselves, then now is the time to take that step. To become fully human, a fully mature adult, we have to choose the set of rules that we want to live by. We need to ask:

Is this family rule really necessary?

Do I need this rule as an adult in today's world?

Do these practices keep me as an adult child, preventing me from growing up?

Does it contribute to healthy and open communication among family members?

What is the teaching of my church on this topic?

Do I want to see my children follow this method in their relationships?

Does this rule help me on my spiritual journey?

Questioning is healthy! It requires a long look at our value system. It forces us to decide if following rules of previous generations is useful today.

As we begin to see how some of these ways of handling life have come down through the family, we will—if we are honest—begin to identify our own negative gifts. All of us have habits, addictions, compulsions, and ways of relating which, like the children in the fable, were given to us. Many of those are unsuited, irrelevant, or harmful, and work against our need for deep communication. Some, such as child and spousal abuse, deny family members their basic human rights. We then teach our children these same ways of relating, continuing the cycles for another generation.

Our most difficult task will be to find the courage for this risk-taking venture. Changing habits and methods of relating is never easy. Unless we take a good look we will never find the peace and stability we search for.

After we learn about our family of origin, evaluate the overall picture of family relationships, and decide which methods of relating are no longer useful, we can choose to change to newer, more productive ways. There are several warnings, however. Deciding to change cannot be done arbitrarily. We need to search out help from the teachings and traditions of the church, from psychological and sociological studies about human nature, and through effective counselling. We need to spend some quiet time discerning God's will for us. Four important steps are necessary for this:

1—Identify what you want to change.

2—Consult with a spiritual director or friends who know you very well or a counselor who can work with you objectively.

3—Read, learn, listen, and pray.

4—Lay it all out for God and say: "Is this what you want me to do?"

If you feel peaceful after taking these steps you can feel confident you have done the right thing. If your decision proves to be a mistake, you can always change. Being human, we do make mistakes, but we can always try again. The very sad thing is to never try.

Communication

Another important step in breaking the cycle of negative gifts is to look at the way family members relate to and communicate with each other. Communication is more than talking about your work, the weather, the latest gossip or today's problems with the kids.

True communication is the sharing of our deepest feelings—our hopes, fears and plans. It involves a whole new way of being honest with feelings—including emotions of anger, jealousy and envy—that is unfamiliar to previous generations.

As we try to improve our methods of communication, try not to judge, blame or project feelings on another family member. Effective communicators use "I"—not "You"—statements. They learn to say: "*I* feel put-down when you shout at me . . ." rather than "*You* always yell at me . . ." They realize that the accusing statements immediately encourage defensiveness rather than promoting deeper understanding.

Changing our ways of communicating is not easy. Those deep childhood habits take time and effort to change. I found Dolores Curran's chapters on communicating in *Traits of A Health Family* and Harriet Lerner's book *The Dance of Intimacy* very helpful.

Although there are books, seminars, workshops and TV programs which can help us work towards this goal, our primary need is for courage and faith. It takes courage to change the ways we approach our loved ones. How will they react? Will they reject us and leave us alone? Putting our faith and trust in our loving God can give us the strength to take the risk.

Positive Gifts

No reflection on our relationship with our parents or how they influenced our lives should dwell solely on negative gifts. So let's take a few minutes to make a list of the positive gifts they gave us. Identify those traits and actions that you want to keep as part of your life.

When my sisters and I get together to look at our childhood, we end up our sessions discussing the positive character traits that we received from our parents. We mention the gift for organization and logical thinking that was dad's way of coping with life, and, to a greater or lesser extent, is part of our lives. His lifelong pursuit of reading and studying certainly had a lot to do with our love of books and theories.

We talk about mom's ability to make new friends and enjoy each person's special abilities and her enjoyment of reading (at the age of ninety-four she still belongs to a book club). Of particular interest to us is her special gift for listening which draws children, grandchildren, great-grandchildren and friends to her when they are grieving over a loss or trying to work out a problem.

All three of her daughters have gravitated toward helping others. One works with the developmentally disabled, another with the divorced, widowed and separated and the last with those trying to overcome addictions and chemical dependency. We smile as we realize "the fruit does not fall far from the tree."

Sheila, Mary and I agreed that all of these parental qualities have shaped us to be the very unique, special people that we are. They are gifts we want to keep as part of our lives. This does not mean we gloss over the negative gifts; it just puts a better balance on our perspective.

In all this talk about our negative and positive legacy, there is one fact we want to keep in mind. Our parents are not "bad people" because they passed on negative behaviors they learned from their parents. Perhaps no one had taught them to be aware of the negative rules of silence, or addictive behaviors, much less given them the tools to change.

The 1990s are a different story. Today the media bombards us with information to help us learn new ways of relating. If we are truly serious about changing, we can find books, audio and video tapes as well as support groups, including twelve-step programs.

We have choices that our mothers and fathers never had. We can break the generational cycle of dysfunctional relationships. It is up to us to decide how to use this time of grieving to make a frank, honest appraisal of our unresolved childhood issues, and eventually make it an experience of learning and growth. As Ecclesiastes tells us, bereavement is "a time for keeping, a time for throwing away." Sometimes it will be a "a time for knocking down," although this review of our past can also be "a time for building. . . ." It is up to each one of us to make the choice.

Taking these risky steps to modify our habits, however, is scary, even if we have help, love and support from other people. This is where our relationship with God proves to be vital. God is waiting to help us. All we have to do is ask.

Everyone who asks receives; everyone who searches finds; everyone who knocks will have the door opened (Mt 7:8).

God gives us the strength to be open to change in ourselves, to try innovative ways of relating to our family and to alter our child rearing practices. Sometimes God speaks to us personally in our prayer and meditation; often it is through others, such as friends, support groups or the various forms of media.

For those of us who are old enough to have grandchildren, we have a special mission to change. If we refuse to keep "family silence" and are open, honest and truthful in answering their questions, we can put a stop to the generational cycle that has contributed to ineffective communication in the family.

Forgiveness and Reconciliation

An old African proverb tells us that "he who forgives ends the quarrel." Depending on our family history, this may be a difficult topic and one which we would like to ignore. Forgiveness, however, is a very basic step in restoring peace and harmony within ourselves and in our relationship with our parents. We must be aware that forgiveness is a process. It doesn't happen all at once.

As we realize the feelings and emotions that surface when we think about our parent's methods of raising children, teaching and discipline, we may find ourselves critical or angry because of our parent's expectations, failings or methods of child rearing.

Did they expect perfection—never making any allowance for age and abilities? Did they demand so much attention that they left us no time to take care of our own growing-up needs? Were we able to express our hopes and dreams to them? Did they allow us to experiment and try out new ways of doing things or did they expect us to follow their directions on how to plan and order our lives? When something went wrong were they there to listen and comfort?

How about those of us who were more seriously abused in our childhood? How can we forgive our parents for physical, sexual or emotional abuse? Forgive a father who devoted more time and energy to alcohol or work or gambling than he did to his family? Forgive a mother who ignored or neglected us? An immediate, likely reaction is "No way!"

Because our parents were human they made mistakes. Frequently they did not know their method of raising children was repressive. They only knew what they had experienced in their own childhood. No one had ever taught them any other way and they passed it on to the next generation.

Even when we understand all this, the fact remains that it is very difficult to forgive when we have been physically or emotionally hurt. We know that all of the abuse was not occasioned by ignorance; some was truly evil. And yet whatever our parent's real or perceived failings, we need to forgive them.

As hard as that may seem, there are several reasons.

We need to forgive because it helps us find peace—in mind, body and spirit. With forgiveness comes healing. To be truly healed, we need to get rid of those emotions which negatively bind us to one another. Recent studies show that there is an organic relationship between our psyche and our body. There is an inseparable relationship between the two and each affects the other. Unresolved anger affects our physical well being. In letting go of anger and forgiving the other, we reduce or eliminate the stress which has the power to make us ill.

Forgiveness makes us fully human. As Christians, we want to be like Jesus who came as a fully human person with an overpowering desire to forgive. Story after story in the gospels tells of his hunger to forgive everyone who asked.

We need to forgive because Jesus said: "If you forgive the faults of others, your heavenly Father will forgive you yours" (Mt 6:14). If we want our sins to be forgiven, then we must forgive the other's sins. To be like Jesus, we need to forgive.

"Forgiveness does not necessarily begin with a feeling; it can begin with an act of the will. To forgive, you do not first have to feel forgiveness. You only have to act on it." This statement from my spiritual director surprised me. So often I felt guilty because I couldn't feel the forgiveness that Jesus said was necessary.

To begin the process of forgiveness, to bring peace into the relationships with our parents (even if they are dead) we can pray with statements like:

I forgive my father for his alcoholic actions and the abuse he inflicted on me as a child.

I forgive my mother for all the times she controlled my life and my actions, not allowing me to decide my own life's direction.

I forgive my parents for the times they didn't listen to me and brushed aside my questions and/or problems.

I forgive my dad for neglecting to spend time with me when I was a child and needed a father's presence.

Perhaps you look at those statements and say: "Under no circumstances can I say anything like that! I can't do it!"

If you aren't ready for that—but would like to be—then start by praying:

Lord, give me the strength to say those words.

Lord, help me to *want* to say "I forgive."

No matter how you feel at the time, saying this is an act of will, an act of forgiveness.

As suggested in Chapter Two, try keeping a journal of your feelings and experiences. Don't be afraid to express your anger. After about six weeks, reread your writing. How do today's feelings compare with those of a month ago? You may have to say your forgiving statement each day for months and months before you begin to feel forgiveness. Don't give up. You are learning to vent your anger in a constructive manner rather than fostering and perpetuating the negative emotion which continues your inner turmoil. If you speak the words of forgiveness with conviction and serenity, eventually acceptance and forgiveness will follow.

This is not easy. It requires long, hard work to become a mature, self-actualized adult, one who can forgive parents for making mistakes, even one who can forgive them for physical, sexual or emotional abuse.

Dennis and Matthew Linn's book, *Healing Life's Hurts* or *Healing the Eight Stages of Life* which they wrote with Sheila Fabricant, can also help with this process.

Be patient with yourself; don't set up a timetable. Just as in grieving, forgiving depends on our life experiences. If we are truly sincere in wanting to forgive, God will give us this grace in his own time.

We take one step at a time: getting in touch with feelings, working through the emotions that have surfaced, finding strength and faith to move along this difficult, long road, forgiving our parents for their mistakes and sins, and finally trying out new actions which conform with the new growth within us. Don't be discouraged. One positive step provides the strength for another.

One young woman referred to this process as a dance. When we learn a new dance step, we take tentative steps together. It may be awhile before we move to the same beat, but we keep trying and eventually we move across the dance floor together. The same is true as we work through grief, looking at the positive and negative aspects of our family, trying to find new ways of communicating with our surviving parent and moving toward reconciliation with those who have hurt us.

Restoring peace and harmony with our parents by forgiving them, even if they are dead, has benefits beyond anything we might expect. We will find a new ability to relate to our children, a peacefulness and tranquility within ourselves, and a deepening relationship with our God.

Confucius has a beautiful saying that has been taught to generations of Chinese.

If there be righteousness in the heart,
there will be beauty in the character.
If there be beauty in the character,
there will be harmony in the home.
If there be harmony in the home,
there will be order in the nation.
If there be order in the nation,
there will be peace in the world.

A Prayer Help

Dear Lord,

You told us in Mark's gospel that those "family secrets" would be brought to light: "For there is nothing hidden, but it must be disclosed, nothing secret except to be brought to light." Give me the light to see my addictions, compulsions, sins and mistakes.

Help me take whatever steps are necessary to change my life and improve my relationships.

I ask for the grace to forgive those who have hurt me and I ask pardon for those I have hurt. In Jesus' name.

Amen.

Five

Prayer
and Spirituality

Yahweh is near to the broken-hearted,
he helps those whose spirit is crushed.

—Psalm 34:18

Prayer can be many things when mourning the death
of a loved one. In fact, it has to be. Our minds just don't
work the same during those first months of bereavement.
We almost seem to put our prayer life and relationship to
God on hold, waiting for the storm to pass. Some of us
automatically continue our routine prayers without even
knowing what we are saying. Others find they cannot pray
at all. Some find comfort from going to church services,
and others can hardly stand to walk in the door. Some of
us are openly angry with God and don't want anything to
do with prayer, church, or religion in any form. Others feel
that the only thing holding them together is their faith in
God.

No matter what your mode of dealing with God and
grief, it's OK—even if you feel guilty about your emotions.
Acknowledge those feelings as part of yourself, and then
decide whether or not your guilt is realistic or unrealistic.
(See Chapter Three.)

After the death of my husband, I attended a support
group which had a poster on the wall:

FEELINGS ARE NEITHER
RIGHT NOR WRONG
THEY JUST ARE!

Feelings themselves are not sinful. They arise from our life experiences. What we do about them, however, is a different matter. The actions that result from those feelings can be either sinful or grace-filled. It is up to us to make the choice.

It does seem as if our lives are full of difficult choices, and we are overwhelmed with the decisions that confront us. Where do we go for help?

Grief can be an opportunity to find God who will help us with those decisions. So often we have to hit bottom before we can admit our helplessness. At that time, the prayer, "Lord, I don't know which way to go. Show me the way!" is all we can utter. That very simple request expresses the longings of our heart more effectively than all the rote prayers we could say. We are admitting our helplessness and asking God, who knows all that's in our hearts, to guide us in the right direction.

Sometimes when we seem unable to pray at all, it is very comforting to remember St. Paul's words: ". . . the Spirit too comes to help us in our weakness, for, when we do not know how to pray properly, then the Spirit personally makes our petitions for us . . ." (Rom 8:26).

We may not even be sure we can count on God to help us, although someplace deep inside, we want to believe. The gospel of Mark tells us about the father of an epileptic boy. When asking for his son's healing, he cried out: "I have faith; help my lack of faith!" (Mk 9:24). Again this prayer may be all we can say, but it comes from the heart.

Most any part of our life can be prayer. Earlier I wrote about journaling—talking to God by writing down our feelings, thoughts and actions of the day and inviting a response to our openness. It helps to write down our prayers of petition. Sometimes we may find ourselves dialoguing with God, writing down our feelings and God's response.

I inherited some dishes and furniture from my grandparents, parents and aunts and just glancing at those tangible objects reminds me of all the positive, intangible gifts they handed down to me before they died. I say a short prayer and ask them to pray for me—making very real the church teaching about the Body of Christ and the Communion of Saints. I know those family members, both living and dead, are supporting me as I travel on my journey to God.

Prayer of Tears

There is a special place in heaven set aside for those who can weep, but cannot pray.

What soap is for the body, tears are for the soul.

These Jewish folk sayings point out that prayers do not need to be words. Edward Hays, author and spiritual director says, "Tears are the prayer beads of us all . . . because they arise from the fullness of the heart." When you think of each tear as a prayer just imagine how many have made their way to the heart of God! Those tears are a special gift from our Creator, expressing our longing for love, comfort and healing. As the Jewish folk saying tells us, they cleanse the soul. A friend spoke for us all when he said: "I just feel better after a good cry. Crying gets the sad out of me."

Crying, is a visible admission of our helplessness. Without any words, tears say: "I can't do it, Lord; I need your help." Members of twelve-step organizations know that the first step in healing is to admit that we are powerless or have no control. If we chose to use the occasion of a parent's death to start on our journey of healing, then these tears are our first letting-go and the beginning of a new way of life for us.

Prayer and Comfort

For a few months after my father died I cried uncontrollably at funerals. I was too busy trying to stop the tears to pray in a community setting for either the deceased or the survivors. I finally realized that I was attempting more than I could handle during those early times of grieving. I learned to send a card or make a short visit to the home initially, then make a longer visit in six weeks or more. I found that a one-to-one basis in a home, I could handle the tears more easily and was often able to pray spontaneously or perhaps read a psalm together.

Frequently there are many visitors immediately after a death, but within a couple of months they taper off leaving the bereaved feeling lonely and isolated. In coming when I am most needed, I not only offer comfort to the bereaved, but also to myself.

If you find that you are depressed or blue a few months after the funeral, don't be afraid to ask a good friend to visit. Tell her/him that you need someone to be with you. Don't be afraid to acknowledge your need for comfort; your friend might just be waiting for a sign that you need help.

Jewish Prayer and Mourning

Jewish traditions and prayers can open up new ways of handling our grief. Since our Christian tradition is based on Judaism, we can use their ancient experience to help us through our grief while reminding us to give glory to our God who is all-powerful, all-understanding and all-comforting.

When a Jew dies, the mourners remain at home for seven days after the funeral (Shiva) receiving condolence calls from relatives and friends. This provides a specified mourning period in which the bereaved have time to deal with the shock of a loved one's death. During the next thirty days (Sholshim) mourners resume work-day activity but avoid places of entertainment. This provides a ritualistic mourning period which allows certain times to be set apart for grieving and, at the same time, encourages them to move slowly but surely back into the mainstream of life. We can use these step-by-step recovery periods to give us a basis for processing our grief during the first year.

Kaddish, a melodious refrain that Jews recite when their loved ones die, is a most beautiful way to honor God and the deceased. The word death is never mentioned; there is only the reaffirmation of the mourners' complete faith in God's goodness, even though the loss of their loved one has turned their lives upside down. The prayer, which is sung at the close of various sections of a congregational service, is recited by mourners on the day of the funeral and continued daily for the next eleven months. The *Kaddish,* an example of which follows, provides a moment of time in each day which is devoted to the loved one's memory, an act of loving kindness and respect.

Mourner's Kaddish

Reader: Hallowed and enhanced may he be throughout the world of his own creation. May he cause his sovereignty soon to be accepted, during our life and the life of all Israel. And let us say: Amen.

All: May he be praised throughout all time.

Reader: Glorified and celebrated, lauded and worshiped, acclaimed and honored, extolled and exalted may the Holy One be, praised far beyond all song and psalm, beyond all tributes which mortals can utter. And let us say: Amen.

Let there be abundant peace from Heaven, with life's goodness for us and for all the people Israel. And let us say: Amen.

He who brings peace to his universe will bring peace to us and to all the people Israel. And let us say: Amen.

On the anniversary of the death, and each anniversary thereafter, the mourners again pray for their loved one, sanctifying God's name and reiterating their trust in the Creator. Because the leader mentions by name those deceased who have no relative present on the anniversary, the memorial prayer assures that the community will not forget them after death.

Kaddish is said only in the synagogue—never alone at home. It is meant to be a community prayer asking for peace to all people, offering praise to God and comfort to each other—a centuries-old support group.

Scripture, Meditation and Contemplation

Probably the most important part of my prayer life, the part that pulls all the other facets together, is my reading of scripture. I look on daily Bible reading as the center of the web which constitutes my life. God's word holds nuggets of wisdom that help me in every aspect of my daily life.

Going over the readings and the gospel each morning puts a special focus on my daily prayer. With an increasing number of lay people I have joined religious men and women in monasteries, convents and churches all over the world in their Morning and Evening Prayers, sometimes known as The Liturgy of the Hours, or Divine Office. The recitation of the psalms and prayers of the prophets, together with the canticles from the New Testament, not only offer praise and glory to the God who made us, but express our feelings when we are angry, depressed, frightened and grieving.

Meditation goes right along with reading scripture. When going through a scripture passage sometimes we come on a quotation that just jumps off the page. It reminds us of a current happening in our lives, or it waves a flag that says: "Stop. Think and pray about this passage!" Spiritual directors advise that we stop right there and reflect on what this means in our life.

For instance, in the eleventh chapter of John we read about Martha and Mary coming to meet Jesus four days after the death of their brother, Lazarus. When Jesus saw the two women and their friends weeping, he was "greatly distressed, and with a profound sigh he said, 'Where have you put him?' They said: 'Lord, come and see.' Jesus wept; and the Jews said, 'See how much he loved him!'" (Jn 11:33-36).

What does this mean in your life? Perhaps you have been so busy spending time with your sick and dying parent, organizing the details of the funeral or helping your own family, you have not allowed yourself to cry. Perhaps you told yourself:

> I can't let go now. If I break down, the whole family will fall apart.

> I never saw dad cry in my whole life; real men don't cry. Therefore I can't let my family see me cry.

> Mother always told me that I was the strong one in the family. If I break down and cry everyone will know how weak I am.

These do not have to be conscious statements but could be holdover rules from childhood. If this gospel passage said: "Stop! Think and pray about this passage," perhaps it is giving permission to have a good cry. If Jesus could weep at the death of a good friend, then surely we can weep at the death of a parent. Often we need that permission before we can let go. Then our prayer is a cry from the heart: "Jesus, I loved my mother so very much! How will I ever get along without her?"

Contemplation, on the other hand, is letting go of every thought, worry and anxiety and just resting in God's presence and love. To begin this emptying we should sit in a comfortable chair relaxing our bodies one part at a time.

I start with my toes, ankles and legs, move through my arms, back, neck and finally the muscles of my face consciously letting go of the tension and stress. This was not easy for me to learn. All the plans for the next ten days, all the "things-to-be-done," plus any worry that was sitting on the edges of my consciousness, managed to parade before my inner eyes.

Finally I learned to be aware of each topic that came into my consciousness, brush it gently aside and go back to an awareness of God's presence within me.

The intrusions happen over and over, but in the meantime I spend some quality time (no matter how fleeting) with the God who loves me unconditionally.

Contemplative prayer makes us aware of the vastness of God's love. God's comfort and compassion offer us healing and renewal during this prayer time, enabling us to find the grace needed to see us through this difficult period.

There are many helpful authors who showed me that prayer is not just saying certain words but can also be a waiting in silence. Their books are listed at the back. I especially recommend M. Basil Pennington's *Daily We Touch Him: Practical Religious Experiences.*

Prayer and Addictions

How can prayer help us when we realize we have received an addiction from a parent who is now deceased? In our helplessness, a simple request, "Lord, release me from this addiction," said from the depths of our being, is a cry from the heart. In making our prayers less complicated, in putting simplicity at the core of our lives, we make progress in calming the chaos that we as addicts have been creating around and within us.

Meditation and contemplation can be especially helpful in praying for release from addictions. In allowing

God to speak to us in quiet and solitude, we receive guidance and help.

Of course we have to act as well as pray. One counselor told me that God answers our prayers by solving 99% of the problem, but only if we act on the remaining 1%. That 1% may mean reading what other people have discovered about addictions and prayer, choosing a support group, taking part in therapy or counseling or, changing our lifestyle (which sometimes means choosing new friends and social occasions). Gerald May's *Addiction and Grace: Love and Spirituality in the Healing of Addictions* may provide new insights for you.

Prayer and Forgiveness

> If you kept a record of our sins,
> Lord, who could stand their ground?
> But with you is forgiveness
> that you may be revered (Ps 130:3-4).

In Chapter Four I spoke of the necessity for forgiveness and reconciliation. Forgiveness, reconciliation, and prayer go hand in hand. In Psalm 130 the psalmist assures us that no matter what we have done, we are forgiven, consoled and welcomed back to God's unconditional love.

We can carry the baggage of anger and unforgiveness with us all our life, but Jesus told us it is not necessary: "Come to me, all you who labor and are overburdened, and I will give you rest" (Mt 11:28). He will help us to let go of the hurt and give it to God. Our forgiveness allows our Creator to fill our newly-emptied heart with love which we can share with others.

Scripture also tells us that we must forgive. Jesus showed this to us:

> Then Peter went up to him and said: "Lord, how often must I forgive my brother if he wrongs me? As often as seven times?" Jesus answered, "Not

seven, I tell you, but seventy-seven times" (Mt 18:21-22).

Rabbinic teaching at the time of Jesus said that God's forgiveness extends to three offenses. At the fourth God punishes. Peter obviously thought he was being extremely generous when he proposed seven times. But Jesus' answer—that there is no limit to the times we must forgive—must have astounded not only Peter, but all those who heard his answer. It still astounds us today.

In teaching us how to pray, Jesus told us to ask God for forgiveness—as we have forgiven those who have hurt us: ". . . forgive us our sins, for we ourselves forgive each one who is in debt to us" (Lk 11:3-4).

An almost certain way for me to forgive someone is to remember that person in my prayers. Almost every month I find myself praying, very often with reluctance, for someone who has hurt me. I prayed for one acquaintance every day for nine months before I could honestly forgive him. The prayer that helped me most was: "Lord, help me see him as you do."

When I saw him recently I knew our relationship had changed, although his personality was much the same. By praying for him, I had put myself at least partially into his shoes, identified his good qualities, and thereby changed the way I saw him. I had grown in my ability to see good in each person—even in one who lashed out hurtfully and viciously when crossed or challenged. God does use evil to bring about a greater good.

Forgiveness consists not only in forgiving a parent who has hurt us, but in forgiving ourselves. Sometimes this proves to be the most difficult aspect of pardoning with compassion. Often we berate ourselves for something we easily forgive in others. We get caught up in "I should have done . . ." a statement that is part of the past and cannot be changed. It is counterproductive in helping us experience life today. Instead of berating ourselves for our mistakes, ask: "What can I do to change the way I react today and in the future?"

Again, a simple prayer that can help us let go of the guilt and forgive ourselves for our sins is "Lord, you have forgiven me. Help me to forgive myself."

We have looked at many ways to pray when we are grieving: with tears, scripture, talking and listening to the loving voice of God, being aware of love, care and concern from other people, forgiveness, a big hug or a tender touch. An awareness of God through his creation—a gentle rain, a robin searching for worms in the backyard, finches at the bird feeder, a pink Flowering Almond bush blossoming outside the window—is another valuable form of prayer.

I have found that two bi-monthly publications, *Praying* and *Living Prayer*, offer me many new insights on prayer. Some articles are written by well-known authors; others are reflections and writings by homemakers, business people, students and religious.

Even while we are in the midst of our grieving—through denial, anger, bargaining and depression—God looks on us with love and gentleness, longing to gather us into his arms and take away the pain. In prayer we allow ourselves to open up and accept God's generous love and the gifts that are waiting for us.

> I shall give them a single heart and I shall put a new spirit in them; I shall remove the heart of stone from their bodies and give them a heart of flesh . . . (Ez 11:19).

A Prayer Help

Dear Lord,

Here I am knowing that I should take more time for prayer, but the thought of adding one more "have-to" to my busy life just scares me to death.

Help me to take five minutes before I go to bed tonight and five minutes in the morning just to sit quietly in silence, listening to your quiet whisper within me.

I need your peace in my life.

I ask this in the name of Jesus, your Son and our brother.

Amen.

Six

The
Surviving Parent

The strong and comforting people
who once nurtured you
are now in need of
your strength and comfort.

—*Earl Grollman, Sharon Grollman*

Those who are grieving often have a hard time focusing their minds and may need assistance with the details of what needs to be done at the time of death. Here is a list of items to be aware of, things that a surviving parent may especially need help with.

1) Decide on the time and place of the funeral or memorial service.

2) Pick a funeral director and determine exactly what the fee includes.

3) If a burial plot has not been chosen, accompany your surviving parent as he or she makes that choice.

4) Make a list of immediate family members, close friends and employer or business colleagues and notify them of the death.

5) Make decisions on flowers and/or appropriate memorial donations; for example to a church, library, school or charity.

6) Write an obituary. Different newspapers have different formats, but you'll need the following basic

information: age, place of birth, cause of death, occupation, educational information, memberships in organizations, military service, outstanding work, and the names of survivors in the immediate family. Give the time and place of the services. The information should be delivered in person or phoned to newspapers. The funeral director may take care of this if you provide him with the information.

7) Notify insurance companies.

8) Arrange appropriate child care. If you have children, be sure to spend time with each, helping them to deal with the death of their grandparent.

9) Consider special household needs like cleaning and food preparation that friends can take of.

10) Arrange for pallbearers. If the men you choose are elderly or have physical problems, they can be honorary pallbearers.

11) Notify lawyer and executor of the will.

12) Plan for the disposition of flowers after funeral— for example to relatives, a hospital, on the grave, or to a rest home.

13) Prepare a list of distant persons to be notified by letter. Often a family group comes up with a more inclusive list.

14) Contact all sources of income such as insurance companies, Social Security, credit unions, trade unions, fraternal and veterans organizations. Inquire about survivor's income from these sources.

15) As soon as possible check on all debts and installment payments. Are there any insurance benefits to cover debts? Consult with creditors.

16) If the deceased was living alone, notify utilities and the landlord and tell the post office where to send mail.

(I am indebted to Judy Tatelbaum, author of *The Courage to Grieve* and Ernest Morgan, author of *A Manual of Death Education and Simple Burial* for some of the information in the above list.)

Very likely you and your siblings will be responsible for encouraging your mother or father to take care of each item on this list. Most funeral directors are also very good at assisting the survivors. It is very helpful to have several people thinking and working together.

If you are helping your mother or father deal with the immediate consequences of their spouse's death, it is important to remember the stages of grief: denial, anger, bargaining and depression. Apply the examples in Chapter Three to your parent.

Your grief and their grief have the same basis, but, because of the different relationship, it will be expressed differently.

The First Few Months

The dynamics of the family undergo profound change at the death of a parent. Relationships between the surviving parent and the children enter a new phase. While they were married, mom and dad were the primary caretakers for each other. Even if the parents had to ask for help as they got older, the children's role was supplementary.

Suddenly the surviving parent can be bewildered and lost, confused about ordinary routines. Dad might need advice on the details of his life, especially when it comes to cooking or keeping house. Mom may panic when it comes to taking care of the car, keeping household appliances repaired or making financial decisions.

Some symptoms surviving parents experience during the first months are:

* inability to make decisions
* confusion
* acting as if nothing has changed
* completely falling apart
* withdrawing into silence

* nonstop talking
* inability to sleep
* crying
* inability to cry

On the other hand your mother or father may surprise you by handling the decisions competently and quickly, falling apart later when the funeral is over and friends and family have returned to their daily routines. It depends on the individual.

Two months after Art and Marie celebrated their 50th wedding anniversary, Marie had a fatal heart attack. Since she died suddenly without symptoms, the children expected their father to be devastated. Much to their surprise, Art voiced definite opinions on the plans and organization of his beloved wife's funeral. He chose the readings, the music, the pallbearers, even the casket. He informed the children he would make no great changes right away, even though two them had invited him to come and live with them.

Six weeks later, however, the children realized that their dad was finally showing his deep grief. The house and yard showed signs of neglect. Often they would drop in for a visit and find he hadn't bothered to fix a meal. He spent most of his days and evenings watching television. He looked haggard and unkempt and signs of depression were prevalent. Other days he would lash out at the children or complain about the doctor who did not find his wife's heart condition at her annual physical.

Art had moved out of denial and was bouncing from anger to depression and back to denial again. This normal behavior showed he was just beginning to realize the depth of his loss. The fears which resulted from this loss were disabling him. Much as it upset the children, their father's anger, depression and pain were signs that he was moving on through the process of grief.

What were the fears that had the power to take away Art's joy of living when Marie died? What were the losses he was unable to verbalize? We can be sure there were one or more, even if he was unable to acknowledge them. On the top of the list was his overwhelming loneliness—a fear that he would be unable to live without her after fifty years of marriage. There may have been fear

* of the unknown
* of the future
* of not having enough money
* of his own death
* of living alone

Each person has his or her own particular list. Contributing to these fears are the loss

* of security
* of trust in God
* of companionship and intimacy
* of a shoulder to cry on
* of a sounding board
* of income

Everything was so new and different. Life had changed in so many ways that Art hardly knew how to proceed.

We should be aware that we need to allow the surviving parent to experience his or her feelings. Don't try to cut them off: "Mom, you have to quit crying. You will make yourself sick."

Allow her to express those feelings, to put into words all those devastating emotions and to cry when necessary. This may take time. Often older parents have had little or no experience in talking about feelings.

We need to allow ourselves time to grieve also. We need to take time and space for ourselves. If the well of our inner self is empty because we have not dealt with our own grief, we will not be able to offer help to the hurting parent. We can only help when our well is full.

Have patience with your parent's progress. Our gentle encouragement, and that of close friends, will help them through this difficult time.

Practical Helps for Later On

We may find our parent extra susceptible to colds, flu, aches and pains. We may observe a sudden aging, a body language that says, "I am getting old!" There may be tears at inappropriate times. Tears themselves are healing, but they can occur at embarrassing times. Here is where our extra compassion and patience is very helpful.

Let your parent decide when to get rid of their spouse's clothes. Some want to do it right away; some find difficulty doing it after six months or a year. Just tell dad, "When you are ready, I will come to help." Don't insist. However, if you see that mom's refusal to give away dad's clothes is a symptom of her refusal to deal with the death, then perhaps some kind of help is in order.

One difficult aspect of widowhood is helping survivors change their routines to fit today's realities. If your father has died, your mother will have a whole new set of worries. She'll express concerns like:

What will I do with the car?

How will I ever learn to balance the checkbook and keep the budget?

Can I mow the lawn and fix the faucet? What if I do it wrong?

Will I be competent to talk to the lawyer? I don't understand legal terminology!

If your mother has died, your father may express concerns like:

How will I ever handle cooking three meals a day?

There is no one to iron my shirts any more! I can't do it!

I don't know how to use the washer and dryer. Who will do that for me?

Mary always balanced the checkbook. Now I'll have to learn to budget.

What kind of a social life will I have? I'm no longer part of a couple.

These concerns result from changes in life structure. The changes however, may be so overwhelming that your parent can't make decisions, and may need help and guidance for a few months.

Time spent right now showing dad how to use the household appliances, helping him shop for nutritious foods and inviting him over for a meal now and then, may be the best thing to help him in the healing process. Encourage him to ask a friend to a concert, movie or sporting event.

Men especially need encouragement that "it's OK to cry!" All their lives they have been told that "Real Men Don't Cry!"

A gentle hug when a tear appears and assurance that everyone needs to cry may be the best gift you can give. Enabling him to try new things for himself can offer dad the love and support he needs to become more self-sufficient.

Mother may need the name of a competent, trustworthy auto mechanic. She might even be open to taking a course on car care given especially for women. That was a big help to me. I couldn't change the oil or rotate tires when I finished, but I knew the routines necessary to keep a car in working order.

Sometimes things pile up around the home: financial concerns, downspouts that need unplugging, faucets that drip, a bush that needs pruning. If we spend an hour or two on a regular basis helping mom or dad we can cut back on the constant telephone calls which interrupt our own routines.

A list of needed repairs or questions by the back door eliminates the nagging reminders that put a strain on parent/child relationships. As you walk in for a visit, you can check the list and say: "I can take care of this one today, mom, but I will have to come back tomorrow (or next week) to do the rest."

With recent studies showing that 10-15 percent of all Americans over sixty suffer from alcoholism, we have to be alert to that possibility.

One-third of all older alcoholics start drinking because of a traumatic loss. These "late-onset" drinkers find that a drink eases the terrible pain they are feeling. Boredom, loneliness and depression have triggered a latent need and they find relief through alcohol. It is easier to take a drink than to go to someone for help in working through their grief.

Alcoholics Anonymous (AA) gives several identifying characteristics of an alcoholic in their pamphlet for older people, *A Time to Start Living*. It warns both men and women that alcoholics are not identified by where, when or how they drink; or by how much or what they drink.

The question that needs to be asked is: "What has alcohol done to me?" If a widowed man plans his days around a drink, if it affects his relationships with family and friends, if he finds himself preoccupied with alcohol, then there is a problem.

A couple of years after my husband died, I found myself very anxious for a drink before dinner. I looked forward to it all day. After all, Jim and I have enjoyed one each night and it seemed to bring out the good memories of our life together. One night my oldest son came in for dinner and challenged me. "Mom, I am quite concerned about you. Every night when I come in for supper you are having a cocktail. Sometimes you even fix another one and have it with dinner. I worry about that!"

I was really shocked, but it did bring me up short and make me aware of my actions. My prayers for the next year asked God to help me get over this one period of the day when I was so vulnerable to taking a drink. It wasn't easy, but Dan's reminder helped me to let go of that reliance.

This applies to prescription drugs as well. Often during serious illness, a doctor will prescribe a tranquilizer or sleeping pill for the spouse. If it is used for too long, that person is at risk, if not already addicted. Children of a surviving parent need to be alert to this possibility and be ready to give feedback to their parent if they feel it is necessary. This can be a time for children and parent to look at addictions and weaknesses that have been passed down for generations. Stories of alcoholic uncles, aunts, grandfathers and other relatives can be an indication that the dysfunctional way of dealing with life's problems has been learned from our parents. It is a time to say: "Do I want to continue acting this way?"

Friends and Social Life

The death of a spouse permanently changes the social life of the survivor. Often the widowed feels like a car's fifth wheel with other couples. Depending on her age and personality, your mother is quite likely to get together with other widows. Your father, however, may have a more difficult time asking other men to go to movies or ballgames. It might help to ask him to join you at an event and encourage him to invite a friend along. Later on he will be more comfortable just going with the friend.

I found that I enjoyed the company of couples a lot more when I found a group of singles for part of my social life. We need to be with a group of like-minded people at least part of the time. Support groups can provide a time and place to meet new people and make new friendships.

Often it is surprising to see which friends stand by when we undergo dramatic life changes such as the death of a spouse or parent. Ann Keiser Stearns writes in *Living Through a Personal Crisis* that "at a time of crisis we are able to distinguish three kinds of friends: empathic friends, basic care provider friends, and destructive people."

She does not characterize the last group as friends—only people! These destructive people are the kind of acquaintances to avoid.

These are the kind of people who start a conversation with a list of calamities, traumas, illnesses and negative judgments about other people. Time with such people is especially difficult for someone grieving over the death of a spouse. Their life needs a positive focus or pretty soon they are down in the dumps and headed for depression.

Other destructive people include those who need to be in control of every situation. Does your father's friend always have to choose the movie or restaurant when they go out in the evening? Does your mother's friend run down everyone's character? Does she continually correct your parent's statements?

Some people also control by appearing weak or helpless. In this way they get their wishes met. Sometimes they cling and allow us no space because being alone frightens them.

None of us need these people. They slow down our process of grieving and prevent us from healing.

Of course we can't choose our parent's friends any more than they could choose ours as we were growing up. We can, however, encourage them to find new interests and new friends. By reaching out for new social activities and learning experiences or spending more time with volunteer organizations our parent can again find a sense of purpose.

If social activities are difficult for your mother, she might like one of the many courses at a community college—cake decorating, creative writing, genealogy, gardening, basic computer, landscaping, assertiveness training—the list is endless. Dad too might enjoy learning new things. Perhaps he has always wanted to visit Mexico. Learning basic Spanish would make his trip more enjoyable. Golf, bridge, introduction to the basics of meteorology, bicycle maintenance and repair are all regular in community college offerings.

Be sure to allow them the time and space for grieving though. Don't try to "cure" them or tell them what to do. Open up new vistas and options with your suggestions but then allow them to make their own decisions.

Financial Worries

Financial worries can and do keep a surviving parent awake night after night. Our surviving parent will benefit from estate and tax planning seminars given by banks and insurance companies. Just a few hours of instruction are especially beneficial for women. They become more familiar with financial terms, gain confidence in their ability to deal with money and those who handle it, like bankers and brokers.

Today we are fortunate to have many sources of help for this. Community colleges offer courses in bookkeeping and budgeting. The American Association of Retired Persons (AARP) offers a Women's Financial Information Program which is designed to help them assess their financial condition and consider options. Concrete advice is given on how much to save, how to invest, how to figure net worth, how much insurance is needed, how much retirement income is available and how to find a lawyer or financial advisor.

If a parent needs assistance with credit counseling, there are many organizations which offer help. For budget planning, or information on health insurance and Medicare, contact the local United Way. It has an information referral program. Consumer Credit Counseling Service offers free tax help to the elderly. Widowed Persons Service is a nationwide program that helps widowed people with everything from support groups and recommended books to social activities and seminars.

Elderly women face special problems with car maintenance and repair. They've lived in an era when the man in the family took care of the car, and he probably never took the time to teach her the basics. Unfortunately there are many people who are willing to take advantage of this ignorance and make some extra money.

Joe's mother-in-law was very concerned about a noise in her five-year-old Buick. Because her recently deceased husband had wondered about the transmission, she took the car to a transmission shop. The mechanic, pointing to a specific problem, told her she needed a new one. Naturally she made an appointment to have it replaced for $850.

After he heard this story, Joe asked if he could have his mechanic check it out, assuring her that a second opinion was always a good idea. The second mechanic test drove the car and added transmission fluid which took care of the problem noise. He assured her that the reason offered by the first mechanic was not valid. Having come from a small town, the widow had a hard time grasping the fact that the first mechanic was trying to take advantage of her.

A month or so later she heard a noise and again was ready to get a new transmission. Again Joe asked his mechanic to look at it. This time it was a vibration in the engine mount which was repaired for $74. Parents do need us when they are encountering new areas of responsibility.

The elderly are very vulnerable to salespeople—either door-to-door or telemarketing. Too often we read about those who have bought a new roof, gutters, downspouts or furnace from someone who showed up at their front door and assured them they needed an immediate repair job. Invariably these operators charge an excessive amount for a shabby repair job and are gone before any complaint can be investigated.

Despite warnings from Better Business Bureau and government agencies, widows sometimes are conned out of their life savings in bogus real estate or investment schemes. Telemarketing and door-to-door high pressure salesmen try to sell investment ideas that "are guaranteed to give a good return!"

One scam operation sends a so-called "bank examiner" to the door asking for help in catching an embezzling employee. "If you will remove $1000 from your account, you can help us catch the thief." The so-called examiner takes the money and the widow or widower is left with a worthless receipt.

The Better Business Bureau says: "If it is 'too good to be true,' it probably *is* too good to be true!" Encourage your parent to deal with responsible home town businesses. Tell them you are always available to discuss any investment or large household repair before they make a decision.

Tender Loving Care

Fathers may not ask for much help but we can be sure that regular times of visiting, calling or inviting them over are an important part of their healing. Dad needs love, companionship and communication with his family. Without that compassion and care, they may move into depression and withdrawal.

Is it possible to offer too much assistance to our parent? Of course. We need to find a balance between no help and too much help. If we wait on mom or dad hand and foot, it is very easy for them to become dependent on us. That could be a source of conflict down the road. We should ask ourselves:

Can mother do this for herself?

Can I do part of it and let her do the rest?

Am I having enough patience to let dad try things for himself?

What is my overall goal? Do I want dad to do as much for himself as he possibly can?

Does this action contribute to that goal?

Above all, we need patience with our parent! Every person moves at a unique pace. However, if we see signs of withdrawal and depression we should encourage counseling. It isn't always possible to get older people to admit their need. In that case, perhaps a session of therapy for yourself or a book geared to grief recovery will surface some ideas. In the back of the book there is a list of those references I found helpful in dealing with problems that arise.

Grief and growth support groups that I recommended in Chapter One are available for spouses. The Beginning Experience Weekend which helps the widowed and divorced work through their grief and shows them the way to closure, was very helpful for me. The Beginning Experience Central Office (address in back) can tell you where to find a nearby weekend.

A final reminder. Don't neglect yourself! Remember that Jesus said we should "love our neighbors as ourselves." Often we forget or neglect our own needs and wonder why there is growing resentment within us. We too are grieving. We need to cry, to focus on our anger, to admit we are depressed. We too, need to be hugged and comforted. Hugs between a surviving parent and adult children can be the basis of a new relationship.

In serving and caring for our parent, we often have mixed emotions. Our own grief may be combined with memories of the deceased parent's strictness, her penchant for controlling us or his physical, emotional or sexual abuse. We can be no help to others unless we take a good look at those feelings. A support group, a twelve-step group or a therapist will give you the time, space and encouragement to move ahead in your own growth.

Coming to terms with our own grief is probably the best gift we can give ourselves, our children and our parent.

A Prayer Help

Dear Lord,

These past months it seems as if I have to make so many decisions for my mother (father).

She (He) talks a lot about what needs to be done, but never quite gets around to doing anything about it.

Please give me the patience to love and support her (him) just as she loved and nurtured me when I was a child.

When my anger seems ready to explode, help me to control my temper.

Make gentleness, kindness and "I'm sorry" my watchwords.

Wrap my mother (father) in your love and walk with her (him) through these lonely years.

Amen.

Seven

Helping Children with Grief

A child can live through anything, so long as he or she is told the truth and is allowed to share with loved ones the natural feelings people have when they are suffering.

—Eda LeShan

Once upon a time there was a little penguin named Fred. Fred's father and mother, like all parent penguins, nurtured, loved, and protected their baby. They taught him how to forage for food, how to keep away from his enemies, how to swim and dive—all things that good penguins teach their children.

After awhile Fred lost his baby fat, grew a new set of shiny black and white feathers and soon was ready to strike out on his own. He found a beautiful mate named Florence and they started their own nest. Before long there were two little penguins, Michael and Debbie, following them around. Life got busy for Fred and Florence and they didn't see too much of Grandpa and Grandma Penguin. They were too busy teaching the children how to swim and dive for their food and how to protect themselves from their natural enemies.

One day the four of them were walking on the beach and they came upon Grandpa walking by himself. Grandpa, with a sad smile, said to the family: "Come and sit down with me awhile. Your Grandma died and I am alone."

Fred and Florence were heartbroken with all kinds of feelings of guilt, denial, loss and even some anger. Michael and Debbie were perplexed. Alone? Grandpa and Grandma were always together! Died? What does that mean? Where did she go? Why wasn't she with Grandpa? Will I die? Will my mom and dad die? If so, what will happen to me?

How do we answer such questions from our children? When grandpa or grandma dies, our children are just as confused as we are—perhaps even more so. They need as much compassion and support as adults in dealing with their loss. But how do we help them when we are hurting so much ourselves? The next few pages will deal with some children's actions and reactions to death, and the concrete things we can do for them.

Understanding our Children

Children feel all the emotions adults feel, but do not have the words to express their hurt and pain, or the experience in communicating those feelings. Parents have to find ways of explaining feelings, beliefs and values so children will understand. Death is likely a whole new experience for them, and they need to know that their feelings and questions are normal.

Children, depending on their age, will react to death in many ways. At first when they are in a state of shock they will have "frozen feelings." As those defrost and confusion begins, they will show anger, frustration, bewilderment, fear, guilt and even depression, depending on the closeness of the relationship with the grandparent. They need to know that their feelings and questions are normal.

Frequently children will regress emotionally to an earlier stage of their development. Younger ones may have trouble with bedwetting, thumbsucking, needing a security blanket, or fear of going to sleep. Older children may show regression in a variety of ways. They may get moody or become very anxious about going to school or camp. They may have violent conflicts with friends and teachers or experience headaches and abdominal pain. Poor grades may surface as the result of lack of attention in school or a tendency to daydream.

Infants, Toddlers and Pre-schoolers

Infants and toddlers are dependent on parents for their total physical care. Since a young child primarily fears being abandoned, the best thing to do when your parent dies is to keep the baby's routine as consistent as possible. Try to provide much loving and hugging to keep their feeling of security intact. When you can't be there, make sure others provide loving attention. Accept the helpful offers of friends to take care of household tasks.

Infants are very sensitive to parent's emotions. If you are nursing, repressing your emotions will affect the production of milk. Talking to a compassionate friend or writing in a journal will help you find serenity.

Because of their strong ties to you, toddlers react to your emotions just as infants do. Child development specialists stress the importance of the parents' love and attention during this formative period. Consistent routine and much loving, petting and holding will provide the needed security and lessen their fear of abandonment.

In a toddler, unlike the infant, the need for security is balanced by the fact the child is taking the first steps to independence. They can sit on a lap just so long before they have to climb down and rush off about their own business. A balance between the two needs of love and letting go is the ideal way for a parent to help the child during this stage. This sensitivity to their needs and a willingness to let them experiment with their independence are especially important in times of household confusion.

Pre-schoolers are learning all sorts of new skills, but basic needs such as security, loving care and stability are still an important part of their growth. During emotional times they can regress in different developmental areas — bedwetting, baby talk, thumbsucking, fear of the dark, need for a security blanket or fear of separation from a parent. Children this age see themselves as the center of the universe and are unable to see another's point of view. Because they can only handle one cause for each event, they may see a grandparent's death as punishment for their naughtiness.

Helps for Parents and Children

How can we help our children with the turmoil they experience when a grandparent dies?

1. Keep to household routines as much as possible. Keep orderliness in their lives.

2. To answer security needs, we should repeatedly say, "I am not going to die; I am not going to leave you," or "you are not alone; I am with you." If you have to leave for a sudden illness or funeral in a distant city, spend some extra time with the child. Explain your plans several times while aware of their ingrained fear of abandonment. Show your love and concern for their feelings. After you are gone follow up with reassuring phone calls and post cards.

3. Explain the funeral and wake ahead of time. Tell them about the service (in simple terms) and what they can expect to happen. Acknowledge that people will be crying and that is the way we all express our sadness about their grandparent not being with us anymore.

4. Be aware that pre-schoolers need explanations in concrete terms. One five-year-old student went to see his grandmother's body before the funeral. Seeing only the top half of her body in the casket, he immediately asked: "Did her legs go to heaven?"

5. Use terms like "dead" and "dying" rather than "sleep," "sleeping with God," "gone to God," "passed away" or "long trip." Here again we must take into consideration children's inability to understand the abstract. If we say: "Grandpa was so good God wanted him in heaven" we might instigate a fear of separation from their parents. Since good people go to heaven, they may choose to be bad and then God won't want them. If we equate death with a long trip the child may worry that dad won't come back from a business trip. If we say: "Grandma has gone to sleep," as one mother did to nine-year-old Sally, we may find our child fighting sleep at night. "If grandma never woke up and I want to wake up tomorrow morning, then I had better not sleep!"

6. Questions and explanations about death and life after death should be based at a level the child can understand, and on your beliefs. The best explanation I've seen for young children comes from *Helping Children with The Mystery of Death* by Elizabeth L. Reed:

A child asks her grandmother, "Nanny, what is death?"

"Wendy, it is when you leave your body," replied her grandmother.

"Oh," said the girl, "no one every explained that to me before."

Reed goes on to say that "it may be necessary to explain further that death means that the body doesn't work any more—the legs don't run, the eyes can't see, the ears can't hear, the heart stops beating; the part of the person that says 'I' has left the body because it could not work any more."

7. Be honest and truthful in your explanation. Lack of simple facts is the cause of many childhood fears. Don't be afraid to repeat these explanations, also, looking at them from more than one angle can be helpful.

8. At this pre-school stage, go to the library and get books that deal with death or frightening emotions. Having stories read to them about other children's feelings can often allay their fears. Sometimes the old fairy tales about giant killers and young people outwitting elders can help allay their fears of not being in control of their lives.

I read Maurice Sendak's *Where the Wild Things Are* over and over again to my two pre-schoolers when their father died. This children's classic validates their fears of wild, scary things in their lives and helps them resolve those feelings so they are willing "to sail back . . . through a day and into the night" of their very own bed at home.

Our children will follow our example in dealing with grief. If we acknowledge our hurt and pain and are open with our feelings, they will do the same. In that way, both parent and child will be healed.

School Age—5 to 12

During these years school age children develop more complex relationships with friends and community. The relationship with their parents is viewed as a deal: "I'll do nice things for mom so she will do nice things for me." They learn verbal, social and physical assertiveness, and sometimes go all out to express this newly-found skill. They think primarily in black and white and either/or categories, unaware of the shadings of grey. They do, however, believe that each person has his or her own point of view and they have no trouble using their newly-found assertiveness to express their opinions.

These developmental characteristics are intensified when grieving. My ten-year-old daughter had trouble with friendships the first year after her father died. She and her best friend had a big fight, calling each other names and refusing to speak to each other. She can remember thinking she had to make a choice—to let go of the friend and go her own way, or to make up with her and overlook the fight. She chose to go it alone. Her concept of right and wrong at that age did not allow for compromises.

When a child in this age group discovers "fairness," he can sometimes carry it to an extreme. We start to hear things like "Joe got a more expensive birthday present than I did!" or "You spend more time with Lisa and her homework than you do with me!"

My eleven-year-old son intensified this preoccupation with fairness after his father's death. He demanded equal portions of everything that the other children received. He would almost weigh or measure it to make sure that everything was absolutely equal, whether it was chicken legs, the size of desserts, or birthday presents.

The reason for this behavior is that he found his life in chaos. Having no control over the death of his father, he would bring order into his upside-down life by controlling what he could, even if it drove the rest of us crazy. This natural developmental characteristic of his age group—to expect equality in all things—was intensified by his grief.

Children of school age are frequently preoccupied with feelings of fear, loss and guilt. There may be a fear of hospitals or illness. If the grandparent died in a car accident, the child may become a "back seat driver" worrying about the parent's driving skills, warning of red lights or a child on a bike.

Children have a basic need to make sense out of what happens. In their quest for understanding, they, like adults, ask "Why?" and unable to answer that question, assume they have been bad or done something wrong. This way of looking at life is the typical "magical thinking" of childhood:

If something bad happens, I am responsible!

I didn't want to help grandma rake the leaves last week. If I had helped, she wouldn't have had a heart attack.

They may think God is punishing them in taking this beloved grandparent away. This unrealistic burden of

WHEN YOUR PARENT DIES

guilt may cause physical illness, accidents or a change in relationships.

Boys and girls of this age are interested in the search for cause and effect, which includes biological aspects of death. Be prepared for questions, questions and more questions, including practical ones about life after death.

Who is going to take care of grandpa now that grandma's dead?

How long does it take for grandma's body to turn to dust?

Will grandma move to a smaller house now that she is alone?

When it rains, will water get in the casket?

How did grandpa get diabetes?

Why did grandpa keep on smoking even though he knew it caused cancer? or

Why do you keep on smoking when you know smoking caused grandma's cancer?

In a child's eyes, these are practical and important questions and they have a basic right to the truth. They learn about death and grief through our example. If we are honest and truthful with them, they will accept death as a part of living.

Basic Helps for School-age Children

How can we help our children? Here are a few suggestions:

* Be patient, especially with emotional regression.

* Provide stability and reassurance. Keep a sense of household routine and order in their lives, but acknowledge the emotional changes the family is experiencing.

110

* Be a good listener and observer. Be aware they are experiencing the same stages of grief as all of us.

* Hug them and tell them "I love you."

* Share your own sadness and feelings of loss with them. Give permission to cry and express their feelings through modeling. If the child doesn't usually cry, let them know it's OK.

* Let them know their feelings are very important.

* Take what you say, and how you say it, seriously. Your words will be remembered a long time.

* Explain that adults have different reactions to death at different times, and the individual child's reactions are their own, special and OK.

* Know that you cannot prevent children from suffering, but you can comfort their suffering and fear by being there when they need you.

* Don't be afraid to say "I don't know." You might also say: "No one really knows why. It's a mystery." or "I'll try to look up the answer and tell you what I find."

* Provide time and space for children to express verbally and non-verbally the images they are forming. This can be encouraged through storytelling, writing or drawing. They are able not only to listen to the stories we tell, but to tell their own with much richness and accuracy. We can learn about their inner feelings through their stories and the pictures they draw. Many children can express with drawings what they are unable to put into words. Art therapists are able to help children deal with scary or inexpressible feelings by helping them to interpret their drawings.

At this age, faith in God relies on the stories, rules and implicit values of the family. This can be a good opportunity to show them how the church community helps us to deal with pain and loss. Share your sad feelings with them and explain that church services and a visit from your pastor were very comforting and helped you deal with the mystery and pain of death.

Adolescents—13 to 18

Adolescent life is so complex. As parents we are aware our teen-agers need to separate from the family, but we worry when they find support through a peer group. We become anxious when they test and reject our value system and form their own.

Adolescents want freedom, but when they realize that freedom must be balanced with personal responsibility, many fears surface. They may feel angry and abandoned by parents and God, causing them to criticize, question and to be less compliant. They tend to spend hours with their friends on the telephone and away from home.

Spiritual development may fall victim to their searching, questioning and anger at those involved in church activities. They may quit attending church, informing us that they "don't get anything out of it."

In today's world they may move quickly into sexual activity, simply because they are eager to experience all aspects of this new life and decide for themselves what to keep and what to throw away. All these normal adolescent characteristics may be intensified and exaggerated when they are grieving.

Teen-agers may grow anxious as they view vulnerable parents. They may withdraw from the family and be unable to cry. On the other hand they may assume more responsibility for chores and decisions, thinking that they need to grow up faster. Each young person is different and will react in different ways.

Basic Helps for Adolescents

We can be most sympathetic to our teen-agers when we appreciate the tensions they deal with. Julie Curry refers to this as "the balancing acts of adolescence," by which teens try to reconcile the tensions of childhood vs. adulthood; stability vs. independence; responsibility vs. freedom; family vs. friends; sexuality as defined in the family vs. sexuality as defined in the peer group; the need for limits vs. the need to test these limits; the reinforcement and feedback from the family vs. that of friends; their anxiety about the future vs. their excitement about it; and the realization that their past has shaped them vs. the desire to create their own lives and identities.

We need to let go of some of the tight controls and allow them to make more decisions within prescribed limits. As much as we dislike it, we have to allow our children to make mistakes so they can learn their own limits and continue to develop and grow to adulthood. This includes allowing them to grieve in their own way. Their experience with grandpa or grandma was not ours; our way of grieving will not be theirs.

Helping them become aware that their feelings of loss or grief are normal; teaching them about Elisabeth Kubler-Ross' stages of grief; and helping them validate their feelings are important parental tasks. Since they are at an age where they may not want any verbal advice, perhaps a book on grieving could teach those things without conflict.

The best and most lasting help we can give our children of any age is to take care of ourselves first. If by example we show that we are dealing with this pain and hurt and are recovering from it, our modeling will teach them how to handle their own grief.

All these suggestions can help our children at what may be their first experience with the death of a loved one. Grandparents and grandchildren have a unique relationship, each filling a niche for the other with very special love, attention and understanding. Be aware of their feelings of loss—but not intrusive. Be there to answer their questions. What they experience will provide a solid basis for dealing with grief and loss as they grow older.

A Prayer Help

Dear Lord,

I feel like I'm squashed in the middle of a three-layer sandwich: mom (dad) on top, kids on the bottom and a thick layer of my own grief plus all my daily routines and obligations in between. I am all worn out trying to take care of everyone. It just can't be done, I know, but where do I stop?

As I take these few minutes with you, show me how to establish my priorities and let go of unnecessary caretaking. Help me to find the courage to say "no" gently but firmly to those who demand more than I can give.

I know that crowds overwhelmed you with their needs, and you had to flee across the lake or up the mountain to renew your relationship with your Father.

Guide me to that place of renewal each day so that I, like you, can help those who need me.

Amen.

Eight

Now and at the Hour
of Our Death

It is the responsibility of the adult children to be sensitive to the inner life of their parents.

—*Mark D. Angel*

Recent medical advances have enabled people who are seriously ill to live longer than they might have a generation ago. We may question the quality of this time, especially if we witness debilitation or some kind of reduced capacity for life in a parent. But we can also look on such time as a gift.

So often after the death of a parent we express feelings of guilt with comments such as: "If only I had told mom how much I loved her" or "I wish I had been able to say 'I'm sorry' to dad before he died."

The gift of extra time allows us to deepen or to heal the relationship with our loved one. How much better to be able to say:

"These last months were a special gift to both of us. We became closer, understood each other better, and were able to show our love for each other."

Such time allows us an awareness of the fragility of life, and to come to terms with our own mortality as we grow closer to our parent and to God. In this chapter I hope to discuss some ideas for easing the stress and tension of such a period of time.

A Changing Relationship

The lifelong, familiar relationship with our parents takes on a different dimension when a debilitating or fatal disease is diagnosed. Putting ourselves in their shoes is the first step in understanding these changes.

Conscious or unconscious fears of suffering, pain, and dying cause feelings of panic and rejection. I have often heard sick people admit they are not afraid of death itself, only of the pain and helplessness that sometimes precedes it.

For many years cancer patients have heard stories of almost unendurable pain and that is all they can think of when they hear the doctor's diagnosis "You have cancer." Patients with heart disease live with the fear they could die of a heart attack any minute, that they will experience unendurable pain, or will lie helpless in bed hooked up to machines, unable to speak or communicate. A person with emphysema who is required to have oxygen available at all times may experience an understandable panic attack because of the horrible fear of not being able to breathe.

Alzheimer patients fear the loss of clear thinking, control of their bodily functions and the inability to continue their life routines. Reason, God's gift to humanity, is being taken away from them and the thought is unendurable. In the early stages of the disease the realization they are having trouble thinking properly or understanding what is going on around them, sometimes causes deep depression. When a close friend with Alzheimer's realized she was losing her ability to think, she told her daughter she was seriously considering suicide. No matter what the disease or illness, each person has unspoken fears which change the way they relate to others.

Parents often try to exert increased control over their adult children by demanding more attention and excessive help with their daily routines. Dad may get grouchy, demanding and stubborn. Mom may demand absolutely everything to be in order, right down to the cover on the bed or the angle of the shade in the bedroom. Having lost control over her life, she is going to rule with an iron hand in any way left to her.

Other symptoms of this underlying fear may be a tendency to manipulate one family member against another or to "play the martyr"—especially if that has proved effective in providing attention earlier in life.

Stages of Grief

Let's take another look at Kubler-Ross' stages of grief—denial, anger, bargaining, depression and acceptance—and see how they might apply to your parent in this situation. It is easier to empathize with the sick and dying if we know the reasons behind their actions—and our reactions.

First of all remember both you and your parents are going through the same process, albeit differently.

Denial

Denial is frequently the first reaction to the news of a life-threatening disease. Some doctors use very little tact or care when informing the patient of the severity of their illness: "You have cancer and can expect to have six months" can be shockingly abrupt. Others are acutely aware of the shock qualities of their announcement and allow both husband and wife time to absorb and handle the diagnosis. No matter how the family is told, no matter how much they have guessed at the severity of the illness, denial and shock will still be their first reaction. Dad may think: "It can't be true! There has never been cancer in my family. I am going for another opinion!" Mom may just ignore everything, fail to tell the family the whole diagnosis, and act as if nothing has changed. "If I don't look at or talk about it, maybe it will go away!" That's OK. God sees that we don't absorb any more than we can handle at one time and helps us to come to terms with our mortality in little steps.

Or perhaps mom refuses to deal with the doctor's diagnosis. It will be easy to get impatient with her reaction: "Isn't she carrying this ignorance thing just too far?" It is true that the ideal parent/child relationship is based on complete honesty, but trying to confront her when she isn't ready, can cause more harm than good. A group of researchers (Schoenberg, Carr, Kutscher, Peretz and Goldberg) in their book, *Anticipatory Grief*, agree. "Much good has come from openness, but it can be overdone." They remind us that not everyone wants to "let it all hang out." We all have limits beyond which we cannot be comfortably open. We should respect our parents limits and tune into their openness.

Eventually we will be aware our parents are moving out of denial. If the sick person gives us an opening such as: "I've been thinking about having my lawyer make up a living will," then we might respond with "that's a great idea, dad. Is there anything I can do to help you with that?" If the occasion seems to be right, you might ask: "Was it hard for you to come to that conclusion?" This would encourage him to be a little more open about his feelings without confronting or prying. Our role is to exhibit patience and gentle encouragement, helping him acknowledge as much as he can right now. Remember each person deals with grief on an individual timetable.

In contrast, if the patient seems stuck in denial for a long period of time, you may want to see if a good friend, or perhaps a trusted priest or minister can establish a rapport which cannot be developed between parent and child. Books or therapists are other sources of help.

Anger

Anger may be directed at the doctor who diagnosed the illness, the nurses who don't show proper care or at life itself for being "unfair." For that matter, mom or dad may lash out at anyone within range. They may be very angry at God but unable to express it. "We were taught that anger was a terrible sin, and now I am dying! I can't afford to admit anger at the God who will judge me very soon!" We shouldn't be surprised if this anger is projected on us. We're handy. God's not!

What can we do to understand and help mom or dad at this time? Because we are a child in our parent's eyes (even though we may be sixty years old) it isn't easy to bring up these subjects. Our suggestions may be ignored, rebuffed or provoke harsh words.

Parents and children alike are afraid to bring up a subject which would arouse feelings of rejection or anger. Both have a great need for love at this time, and don't want to do anything to damage the relationship. As a result we sometimes ignore the whole thing, assuring ourselves that "mom isn't ready to talk about it yet."

That may be true, but we should keep our eyes open for changes in attitude. We may find the opportunity to help mom be more open and honest with her feelings. When we admit that we are experiencing anger at God because of their illness, we give loved ones or friends permission to acknowledge their own feelings.

Perhaps a visit from a pastor could open a new way of seeing this anger. A pastoral minister is usually a good listener, one who can help us and our parent direct our feelings and teach us new ways of dialoguing with God.

Probably the most loving thing we can do is visit frequently, and become a compassionate listener by allowing our parent to talk about whatever needs to be aired. Just knowing they have a sounding board can assist them along this difficult road.

Bargaining

Bargaining is common for someone in a long term illness. We hear statements like, "Just let me stay alive until my youngest daughter is married," or " Lord, take this cancer away until my children are grown."

Bargaining is a form of controlling. A parent may have moved out of the denial stage, but is not ready to give up all control on how and when he or she will die.

Bargaining was very evident when a good friend informed her family that she was ready to go, but wanted only certain friends and relatives with her when she died. She asked these people to be with her on a certain night which she had chosen, "knowing" that God would take her on that particular date. "I'm ready to die, God, but I want to chose the time and place!" When she woke up the next morning, her bargaining was done. She was very, very angry. God hadn't taken her after all!

During the next two weeks we saw my friend alternate between anger and depression. Finally, a peacefulness settled on her features in her last days. When death came, she had a soft smile on her face. She was able to let God take charge.

The dying parents might be tempted to think he or she is dialoguing with God, but the conversation is more of a monologue, telling God what should be done and how to do it.

Depression

As dad looks back on his life, he may see all the mistakes he has made, all the people he has hurt, all the sins he has committed, and depression sets in. Mom may feel that she has accomplished nothing worth remembering, and she too will experience depression. Neither feeling may be valid, but feelings are not right or wrong; they just are.

Our job at this point is to understand those feelings and assure them of our love, even though they have not been perfect. We need to assure them that God loves us just the way we are. God forgives and forgets all our sins and failings, waiting only to welcome us home with open arms.

Acceptance

Acceptance is marked by peace and contentment in the face and manner of the person facing death. There will be a realization that he or she has let go of the control of life, showing trust in God's ultimate love and goodness. By this modeling they can teach us to do the same.

Not everyone reaches that stage of "letting go" to those around them. Some fight everything that life has to offer them, and won't change in the face of their final illness. Be assured that God understands them better than we do. We find our faith in a God who, according to Psalm 139, has searched us and known us from our conception in our mother's womb to this very day. God will see that each one of us "will follow not the wrong way, and will lead us in the way of life eternal."

Ethical and Moral Dilemmas

There is a season for everything . . .
A time for giving birth, a time for dying (Eccl 3:2).

My mother often comments on the revolutionary changes of her lifetime. In those ninety-five years we have experienced an exponential leap in scientific knowledge, contributing to better health and longer life. Even some diseases have been eliminated. When my mother was born in 1897 a woman's life expectancy was forty-nine years. Today's young woman can expect to live eighty-three years. To the people of the early 1900s, our ability to stave off death would be as unthinkable as a trip to the moon.

However, we are confronted with ethical and moral dilemmas that our grandparents never had to face. During the past few years much legal and media attention has been paid to such items as living wills and durable powers of attorney. The courts are increasingly insistent that some document listing the patient's wishes be available before the removal of life-sustaining machines can be permitted.

Today many hospitals give a patient facing serious illness an Advance Directive along with a booklet explaining what it is. This legal document states health care choices and allows the patient to name someone to make the choices if the patient becomes unable to do so. Making such a decision at this time only adds to an already stressful situation. It would be much easier on everyone if such decisions were made before an illness sets in.

The way to do this is through a Durable Power of Attorney and/or a Living Will. A Durable or Medical Power of Attorney is a document through which another person is named to make health care decisions for someone who is unable to make them. A Living Will, on the other hand, is a directive to a physician which gives permission to have life-sustaining procedures withheld or withdrawn in the face of terminal illness.

Most attorneys encourage the first because it names an agent and gives him or her the power to make a decision with the latest information. For example, as your parent's agent, you can make an intelligent and loving decision based on the most current medical knowledge, the physician's recommendation and the help and support of your church community. If this is done before a serious illness, it takes pressure off the whole family and enhances good family communication.

Attorneys, hospitals and nursing homes should have the information necessary to proceed. Both documents can be tailored to the specifications of the parent and preclude much anguish and family discord as well as potential legal hassles.

Parents will need plenty of time to deal with the grief that goes with signing these documents. It is scary to have to give someone else legal power to end our life, even when that person is a loving and caring child. Mom or dad might even have to deal with some or all of the stages of grief before signing them.

One of the most difficult parts of care-giving is having to decide whether or not to start, continue or end extraordinary methods of sustaining life. It is heart-rending to say: "No more treatment." It is especially heart-rending when we have to make a decision about our parent's "quality of life." How much care is "too much"?

How do we decide when the financial cost is more than anyone can handle?

No one has any pat solutions to this dilemma. I can only relate how I tried to handle this problem in my family. My 93-year-old aunt, who died last year, had given me power of attorney for financial affairs and her health care. I read as much as I could about health-care ethics and talked with doctors, hospitals, nursing home staff and pastoral ministers about our options.

Although she could neither eat nor breathe without mechanical help, Aunt Mildred was alert and able to make decisions on her own. She did, however, need time to work through her feelings about extending the extraordinary treatment. She was also quite concerned that refusing such treatment would be suicide. She needed to talk over the decision with me and with her professional care-givers.

Without making the decision for her, I explained her choices as best I could and called her pastor to come in and talk to her about the difference between extraordinary care and suicide. With compassion and gentleness he explained: "Sometimes, Mildred, God gets a little upset with us because we try to decide when we're going to die. We try to keep control—and really God is in charge. He says to us: 'It's time to come to me,' and by our actions we say 'Not yet!'" He explained that the church does not expect us to use extraordinary means to stay alive when there is no hope for a recovery.

Within the hour, she made the decision to let go. I, too, was ready to let go and lift my beloved aunt to God in prayer. It was not easy. But because I believe in life after death, I have the comfort of knowing that Aunt Mildred has left a life of intravenous feeding and tracheal tubes and has found happiness and peace with the God who loves her so very much.

Before making such a decision however, I again suggest checking the legalities. Doctors, pastors, nursing home and hospital administrators can all help in this regard.

Nursing Home vs. Home Care

The decision to use a nursing home is a wrenching one. But we do not have to make the choice alone. Learning about our options is the first step. Here are a few suggestions:

1) Consult with the doctor about the disease and the problems the patient faces in the coming days.

2) Spend some time deciding which option you feel is best for your parent and for you! Choosing a nursing home does not constitute neglect; you are not necessarily trying to get out of your responsibilities. For example, if you are working full time and taking care of a family, are you able to add these other duties?

3) As your research progresses, share information and ideas with siblings and the healthy parent if there is one. The decision does not have to be yours alone—in fact, family relationships will benefit if a consensus is reached. Keep in mind each person has a different agenda because their relationship to the parent is different.

4) If you are the prime care-taker, dialogue with your brothers and sisters, telling them of your fears and anxieties. Ask if they can be counted on for emotional, financial and physical support when needed. Talking about this at the outset, before you collapse in exhaustion or anger, can deflect many family arguments.

5) Research local nursing homes. Check books and pamphlets in your library for guidelines on choosing a place to care for your parent.

6) Establish a criteria and visit several homes. Get honest opinions from other families who have relatives in the homes.

7) Investigate hospice care. Many people have heard of this but don't know exactly what it is. *The Hospice Way of Death* explains the concept: "Hospice is a program which provides palliative and supported care for terminally ill

patients and their families—directly or on a consulting basis. The emphasis is on symptom control, preparation for and support before and after death." Hospice movements all over the world are devoted to helping families bring their loved ones home instead of having them die in sterile atmospheres.

Working with the doctor, hospice workers see that the patients have medication to relieve pain and equipment to make them comfortable. The assistance is offered for any dying patient, no matter what the disease.

Hospice also provides a listening ear and valuable tips to the care-taker, while providing respite from the demands of care-giving. For example, when my aunt was dying, a hospice worker stayed with her while my daughter and I went out for a breakfast.

8) Check with hospitals or health care organizations for information on at-home health care. Often county nurses will check patients in rural areas on a daily or weekly basis.

9) Run newspaper ads or ask friends for information on live-in or daily household help. Although most of the time this is difficult to find, there are some people who will do light housework and fix one meal a day for your patient.

10) Find a support system. Outside of finding a doctor who will take care of your parent's medical needs, this will be your biggest need as care-taker. You need information about the disease, ideas for helping you and your parents with their daily routine. Most importantly, you need a listening ear when life's problems seem overwhelming. Many groups exist to help support those involved with long-term illnesses. These include the National Alzheimer's Association, American Cancer Society, Multiple Sclerosis Society, and the Arthritis Association.

The local newspaper is a good source. Often it will publish weekly reminders of groups which meet periodically. Sometimes newspapers have a whole section devoted to the names, addresses and telephone numbers of national organizations who will refer you to local groups. Most of them have 800 numbers. Local mental health associations and area hospitals are also good sources of information. A list at the end of the book provides additional help.

Prayer—Intimacy with God

Jim Scully, author of *You Can Be Real With God*, says the purpose of all prayer is to be intimate with God. This intimacy can open a new aspect of prayer which will support us when we are faced with the illness and impending death of our parent.

No matter what we were taught as children and adolescents, today we can go to our God who will understand our feelings and comfort us as a mother comforts her hurt child. God wants to be intimate with us, to have a personal relationship with us, to be the mother and father that our human parents could never be.

True intimacy with God requires openness, honesty and acknowledgement of both positive and negative feelings. Intimacy with God enables us to pour out all our troubles, fears, frustrations, anger, exhaustion, loneliness and sadness. Like the loving and understanding father in the parable of the Prodigal Son, God's arms will be open wide in welcome. Only when we are able to reveal everything that is bothering us, will God's healing love help us.

There are numerous methods to use, but to get started I like to find a quiet prayer corner. My favorite spot is an old rocking chair in my bedroom. Relax your body and identify some of the emotions you are feeling.

Do you find anger, frustration, fear, anxiety? Are you depressed? Are you worried about the financial aspects of your parent's illness? Are you physically exhausted with your role as care-taker? Are you lonely?

Now let your memories wander back in years to your childhood. How did your family deal with these emotions? Did they deny and ignore them? Did the family rules hinder expressing those emotions? Or did they encourage openness and acknowledge that every person had those feelings one time or another?

Sit silently in God's presence, share yourself, and listen to his Word. Prayer, woven in and out of each of the above guidelines, will be the warp or essential fiber of your decisions in difficult times.

Finally intimate prayer is pouring out our thankfulness, gratitude and joy to the one who has helped us through our difficult moments so far and will not desert us now.

A Prayer Help

The prayer of Dietrich Bonhoeffer, the Lutheran pastor who was executed in a Nazi concentration camp, will help us through the difficult days.

O heavenly Father
I praise and thank you for the peace of the night;
I praise and thank you for this new day;
I praise and thank you for all your goodness
and faithfulness throughout my life.
You have granted me many blessings.
Now let me also accept what is hard from your hand.
You will lay on me no more than I can bear.
You make all things work together
for the good of your children.

Amen.

Nine

Go with God

Go into the light
and do not look back.
We will care for everything here.

—*Cheyenne Native American Prayer*

Although my father died twenty years ago, I found myself reminiscing on a recent birthday of his, still trying to say goodbye. I thought of my growing-up years, when he would read the "funny papers" to me using the occasion to teach me to read. I thought of the one time he spanked me—when I had lied to him. I thought of the many nights he walked to meet me as I came home from being with teen-age friends. My hometown had a military air base and he never let me walk alone at night. I thought of the times he tried to interest me in economic theories—the love of his life.

I wondered what part of him became a part of me. My most formative years were spent with this man, and I must have absorbed some of his values, goals and ways of dealing with life. Recently I told one of my children that my dad drove me crazy as a teen-ager trying to interest me in Henry George's economic theory and Pope Leo XIII's encyclical *Rerum Novarum.*

He was convinced that only by following their recommendations would the world eliminate inequality, hunger, homelessness and refugees. Today I find myself writing letters to newspapers, senators and representatives encouraging them to use the peace dividend to help the hungry, homeless and those who flee repression in their native land. "The fruit does not fall far from the tree."

I regret the distance that separated us as I raised my family half a continent away, allowing dad's grandchildren the joy and comfort of his presence for only a week or two at a time. Have any of his attributes been passed down to my children and grandchildren?

I look at my own adult children and see one who not only looks like my father, but approaches life with his calm and thoughtfulness. Another has his asset of attention to details and logical thinking that drove me up the wall during my teens. My year-old grandchild resembles my father's sister, although they were born ninety-two years apart. My father's spirit has not died. It lives on in his children, grandchildren and great-grandchildren.

Even when we know that our parent is not gone forever, we still have to accept our temporary parting. But we need to take this knowledge out of our heads and make it concrete. This is called ritualizing, performing some physical act that integrates this knowledge into our inner beings.

Funerals

From the beginning of time we have used ritual to help make sense out of suffering and death. The primary ritual, the beginning of our grief work, is the funeral. For Christians this includes not only the rite of burial, but also the anointing of the sick and the wake. The Jewish rituals, *Shiva*, *Sholshim* and especially the *Kaddish*, unite the living generation with the one that has gone on before, while encouraging the survivors to let go of their loved one.

Because we don't really understand why our loved ones die, we ask "what is the meaning of death?" or "why does it happen?"

The funeral rites, formed through the centuries by millions who have struggled with the same questions, help us act out our response to these mysteries. They help us through the first shock of grief. The comfort and compassion shown by friends, co-workers and relatives help cushion our feeling of abandonment. We need to hold on to the important truth that we have others to help us through our bereavement.

Ritual in Everyday Life

There are other, smaller rituals to help us close the door on our past life and get on with the future. Some will help heal our personal sores, and some are designed for family healing.

One suggestion is to write a letter to your dead parent.

Don't laugh! It's for your benefit. Write about your loneliness, anger, worries, conflicts, problems—whatever is part of you at the moment.

You might want to include personal thoughts and reflections which for whatever reason, you were never able to share when your parent was alive. Perhaps you need to tell them about your happy memories—how you enjoyed the trips, the family picnics and reunions, the different houses you lived in, even some school incidents that you and your siblings had kept secret.

You could tell them of the characteristics and ways of dealing with life that they handed down to you and to your children. You might want to reflect on the differences between the three generations, showing how each has learned to handle life in its own particular way. Susan Richards Shreves's novel, *Daughters of a New World*, offers a fascinating look at this development in the saga of a four-generation family.

You may want to write one letter early in your grieving period and six months later write another. This will help you see how you have grown. As you work through your grief you might want to write a letter of closure allowing yourself to let go of your parent. Your letter can express your love and forgiveness, acknowledge their positive teachings. The letter will offer you a way to gently close the door on this part of your past.

No one has to see these letters, but you might consider keeping them as mementoes for your own children when they mature. They will learn more about their parents and grandparents. Letters written by previous generations can be a special form of love and learning for generations to come.

When the time comes to clean your parent's house, make sorting out the accumulations of a lifetime a family affair. Invite your siblings to come and join you. As you itemize and organize those items which were important in your growing-up years, tell each other what you remember about your childhood, some of the escapades you got away with and some that you didn't. Not all of our stories will be happy ones. Some of us may admit we were hurt in childhood and we may hold a grudge against a parent or sibling. This time, however, can be used to let go of past offenses, acknowledge mistakes, apologize for any pain caused and forgive the hurts. The family bond, broken over the years, will begin to heal. Even if there has been no open hostility, working together and sharing insights and stories, both good and bad, will strengthen family ties.

A few months after my widowed mother-in-law died, her three daughters-in-law got together and began to clear out the house which my husband's father had lived in since he was born. Trying to decide which items to keep, which to pass down to the grandchildren, which to donate or sell took many hours of hard work. Because three of us were working together, the time was enjoyable and passed quickly.

Comments about this piece of furniture and that dish or knickknack stirred memories about the early years of our marriages. When our husbands came to help us, they joined in our reminiscing. We were able to end the days with thankfulness for all that Joe and Lois had contributed to our lives. It was a way of saying goodbye.

There are other ways to help your family through grief. Several years ago, my friends' youngest son was murdered. The first night the family was together they talked about their depression, guilt and especially their anger—at the murderer, at the doctors and nurses who failed to save him, at God for allowing this to happen to a twenty-three-year-old. They were even angry with themselves for whatever guilt they were feeling at the time. They were encouraged to vent their feelings within the safety of the family circle.

The next night they talked about the gifts their brother had given to the family—his love of people, his ability to get a party together at a moment's notice, his sense of humor—all things that had taught them to enjoy life's present moment. His gifts had influenced them to become better people, and by the time of the wake and funeral, they were ready to express this to their friends in the eulogy and homily at the funeral. This was their way of saying goodbye.

Sometimes these goodbyes are said months or years after the actual death. Whenever the family gets together—Christmas, Thanksgiving, summer vacations— is a good time to reminisce, forgive, love and bring closure to an aspect of the relationship.

Children's Goodbyes

Children need to ritualize their goodbyes just as adults do. They are innately creative, and someplace deep inside, that creativity waits to be loosed. Since young children are unable to verbalize their feelings, they can be encouraged to express their emotions through drawing. Have them tell a story of their drawing in order to get some insight into their feelings. It even helps adults.

I recently made a six-day retreat in which I tried to get in touch with my inner child. My retreat director had me get crayons, paints and drawing paper, told me to express myself by drawing pictures, rather than writing words. This was quite an assignment for a woman who hadn't painted or drawn since grade school, but I was surprised to see how it freed up a lot of feelings—even in this grandmother.

Grade school children are quite adept at writing stories which will help them remember happy and sad times with their grandparent. At the same time, they are becoming more and more proficient with computers. Encourage them to use a word processor, to write or print a letter to their grandparent. They might want to tell grandpa or grandma all that is happening in their life right now, how much they miss them, and say goodbye—if they are ready. It's OK if they don't wish to show the letter to you. Allow them the privacy you would give an adult.

Sometimes long walks with teen-agers, talking with them about our own memories will help them to deal with their mixed-up feelings. When my children were adolescents, we had a hard time talking to each other. I finally learned that when I really wanted to communicate with them, or share some of my feelings and ideas, I had to write them a letter which I would then put on their pillow while they were in school. This gave both of us time and space to think out our responses.

Writing to share your thoughts, ideas and reflections about the death of your parent in effect gives them permission to look at their own thoughts and feelings.

Family History

Researching the family history can be fascinating as well as healing. How many stories of our parent's growing up can we remember? Did our parents live all their lives in one area of the country? Did they travel a lot? Where did our ancestors come from? Did mom or dad's parents or grandparents emigrate from a foreign country? Has anyone ever written down our parent's story? Or narrated it onto a tape recorder?

If mom is still alive get her to tell about her life in relationship to world events of her time. If dad was in the military during a war, get him to relate his experiences. Perhaps mom can reminisce about her childhood in a large city or dad can tell about life on a farm. Sometimes they can tell stories about their ancestors' lives. These oral histories should be recorded for future generations. In these days of the camcorder, and audio cassette, what a priceless gift for your children and grandchildren! Knowing more about their forebears from true-life stories gives us all insights into feelings and actions.

One family I know planned a reunion at a lake campsite the summer after their mother died. Their father had died ten years earlier. Each son or daughter was asked to bring one or more outstanding memory or story to share. They had expected the children would swim and play while the adults would rest, reminisce, share their grief and tell their stories to each other. Surprisingly the grandchildren provided and added dimension by telling their own stories. The whole family was able to say good-bye and put closure on that part of their life.

Your History

Have you ever thought that before too long you will be the source of history for your children? Your life as a child, adolescent and young adult is pretty foreign to young people growing up today. Society has changed exponentially, making it difficult for them to visualize what life was like thirty or forty years ago.

Use old photo albums, snapshots and formal portraits. They will stimulate recollections of trips, family get-togethers and holidays. Long-forgotten memories surface.

To end your story you might comment on the values and goals you were taught as a young person and reflect on their suitability for the future. Perhaps you would keep the same values and goals, but find different ways to reach them.

Taking Risks

Life is full of risks and most of us hesitate to put ourselves in a position of being hurt. But always, our Father keeps calling to us. Jesus answered "Yes" to God's call to risk and suffer; now we are called to risk and perhaps suffer rejection, pain and hurt. The realization that we need to love, help, and forgive others is scary. Trying to relate to others in a new way is risky and scary.

When my parents were in their late fifties they pulled up stakes in their native South Dakota and moved to California. It certainly couldn't have been easy since they had a twelve-year-old girl and dad had no job. He had been stationed there in World War I and fell in love with the state. After World War II, they sold their home and started out on a new adventure.

By this action my dad and mother taught me an important lesson—learn to take a chance. They left security behind and trusted that God would care for them. God did take care of the family and dad thoroughly enjoyed his years in the Golden State.

When I was a little girl I was afraid to take risks, afraid to try new ways of doing things, afraid of being different from everyone else. Although it took me many years to overcome this childhood fear, God never stopped calling me. There is an old saying that "the person who risks nothing, has nothing and is nothing."

I once took the risk of exposing my deep feelings to a small group of people who had been hurt as I had been hurt. I was astounded at the freedom I felt, at the love, empathy and forgiveness that was evident in that group. No one judged me; no one was shocked. They understood and loved me. In that room God touched me with unconditional love, just as these people did. I knew that I did not have to be afraid to try new things, to reach out to others, to love again and again and again.

How will rituals and risk-taking help us say goodbye to our mother or father? They teach us we are no longer children.

We are adults with life experiences of our own, living in a different era from our parents, and with the intelligence and knowledge that we can make decisions suitable for today.

We will be able to say:

> I appreciate all you taught me. You did the very best with what was available at the time, but now it is time to move on. I am not casting aside what I learned from you, but I am adding my own experiences, realizing that both are necessary. I will make mistakes, just like you did, but with God's help I will grow closer to my Creator and follow his will more closely. Your love for me and my love for you will be the foundation I build on in constructing my future growth and development. Thank you for all you gave me.

I find it difficult to say goodbye to my father. Even though I know that originally "goodbye" was a contraction of "God be with you," the word sounds so permanent, so final. So much is left unsaid between us, so much left to learn about each other. Yet I have the consolation of knowing that the one talk we had just before he died (related in the introduction) gave me a foundation for building my life after my husband died. What gift could be more valuable? It is my hope that I can do the same—leave a solid foundation for the next generation.

Finally I am able to say "go with God." I can let dad go to the one who loves him unconditionally, knowing that death is not the end of our relationship. In the meantime, I have things to do and roads to walk. I have risks to take and people to love. We all do.

My prayer for you as you continue your journey is:

May Yahweh bless you and keep you.

May Yahweh let his face shine on you and be gracious to you.

May Yahweh show you his face and bring you peace (Nm 6:24-26).

A Prayer Help

Lord God,

Like the old song,

> "Ev'ry time we say goodbye I die a little.

> Ev'ry time we say goodbye I wonder why
> a little."

I know part of me dies when I have to say goodbye
to those I love.

But I also know that the same part of me rises again
to a new life.

> Each time I look back on my losses, I realize
> that working through that grief and sorrow
> has brought me closer to you.

> Please give me the faith to believe that, in
> the fullness of time all will be well.

> Give me trust-filled hope that I will see my
> loved one again.

> Above all give me love enough to help my
> brothers and sisters through their grief
> and sorrow.

I ask this through the intercession of all those who
have lived through this dark night.

Amen.

Reading and Reference List

Books

Grieving

Angel, Marc D., *The Orphaned Adult: Confronting the Death of a Parent*, New York: Insight Books, Human Sciences Press, 1987.

Brothers, Dr. Joyce, *Widowed*, New York: Simon and Schuster, 1990.

Kubler-Ross, Elisabeth, *On Death and Dying*, New York: Macmillan, 1969.

Kubler-Ross, Elisabeth, *To Live Until We Say Goodbye*, Englewood Cliffs, NY: Prentice-Hall, 1978.

Kubler-Ross, Elisabeth, *Working It Through*, New York: Macmillan, 1982.

Nongesser, Lon G., with William David Bullock, *Notes on Living Until We Say Goodbye: A Personal Guide*, New York: St. Martin's Press, 1988.

Price, Eugenia, *Getting Through the Night: Finding Your Way After the Loss*, New York: The Dial Press, 1982.

Schoenberg, Carr, Kutscher, Peretz, Goldberg, *Anticipatory Grief*, New York: Columbia University Press, 1974.

Stearns, Ann Keiser, *Living Through Personal Crisis*, Chicago: The Thomas More Press, 1984.

Tatelbaum, Judy, *The Courage to Grieve*, New York: Harper and Row, 1980.

Family Relationships

Berne, Eric, *Games People Play: The Psychology of Human Relationships*, New York: Ballantine, 1973.

Bradshaw, John, *Bradshaw On: The Family: A Revolutionary Way of Self-Discovery*, Deerfield Beach, FL: Health Communications, 1988.

Curran, Dolores, *Traits of a Healthy Family*, San Francisco: Harper, 1985.

Friedman, Edwin, D.D., *Generation to Generation: Family Process in Church and Synagogue*, New York: The Guilford Press, 1985.

Koch, Tom, *Mirrored Lives: Aging Children and Elderly Parents*, New York: Praeger, 1990.

Leman, Dr. Kevin, *The Birth Order Book*, New York: Dell Books, 1985.

Lerner, Harriet Goldhor, *The Dance of Intimacy*, New York: Harper and Row, 1989.

Shreves, Susan Richards, *Daughters of a New World*, New York: Doubleday, 1992.

Addiction/Codependency

Beattie, Melody, *Codependent No More*, New York: Harper/Hazelden, 1987.

Bradshaw, John, *Homecoming: Reclaiming and Championing Your Inner Child*, New York: Bantam Books, 1990.

May, Gerald G., M.D., *Addiction and Grace*, San Francisco: Harper, 1988.

McCall, Peter, OFM Capuchin, *The Healing of Codependence*, Pecos, NM: The Pecos Benedictine, Dove Leaflet, 1991.

Schaef, Anne Wilson, *Co-Dependence: Misunderstood-Mistreated*, New York: Harper and Row, 1986.

Schaef, Anne Wilson, *When Society Becomes an Addict*, San Francisco: Harper, 1987.

Wegscheider-Cruse, Sharon, *Choice-making: for co-dependents, adult children and spirituality seekers*, Pompano Beach, FL: Health Communications, Inc., 1985.

Healing

Linn, Matthew, and Dennis Linn, *Healing Life's Hurts: Healing Memories Through the Five Stages of Forgiveness*, New York: Paulist Press, 1988.

Linn, Matthew, Sheila Fabricant, and Dennis Linn, *Healing the Eight Stages of Life*, New York: Paulist Press, 1988.

Shlemon, Barbara, *Healing the Hidden Self,* Notre Dame, IN: Ave Maria Press, 1982.

Children .

Jewett, Claudia L., *Helping Children Cope with Separation and Loss*, Boston, MA: The Harvard Common Press, 1982.

Kubler-Ross, Elisabeth, *On Children and Death*, New York: Macmillan, 1969.

Reed, Elizabeth L., *Helping Children with the Mystery of Death*, Nashville and New York: Abingdon Press, 1970.

Rogers, Fred, *Talking With Young Children About Death*, pamphlet, Pittsburgh, PA: Family Communications, Inc.

Sendak, Maurice, *Where the Wild Things Are*, New York: Harper Trophy, div. of Harper/Collins, 1963.

Final Illness

DuBois, Paul M., *The Hospice Way of Death*, New York: Human Sciences Press, 1980.

McAndrew, Lynn, *My Father Forgets*, Maple City, MI: Northern Publishing, 1990.

Morgan, *A Manual of Death Education and Simple Burial*, Burnsville, NC: Celo Press, 1977.

Munley, Anne, *The Hospice Alternative*, New York: Basic Books, Inc., 1983.

Oliver, Rose, Ph.D, and Frances A. Bock, Ph.D., *Coping with Alzheimer's*, North Hollywood, CA: Wilshire, 1989.

Prayer

Bergan, Jacqueline and S. Marie Schwan, *Forgiveness: A Guide for Prayer*, Winona, MN: St. Mary's Press, 1985.

Finnerty, Rev. D. Joseph and Rev. George J. Ryan, editors, *Morning and Evening Prayer: Selections from the Liturgy of the Hours*, Collegeville, MN: The Liturgical Press, 1985.

Hamma, Robert, *Come To Me*, Notre Dame, IN: Ave Maria Press, 1993.

McNally, Thomas, C.S.C., and William G. Storey, D.M.S., compilers, *Lord Hear Our Prayer*, Notre Dame, IN: Ave Maria Press, 1978.

Nouwen, Henri J.M., *A Letter of Consolation*, San Francisco: Harper and Row, 1982.

Pennington, M. Basil, *Daily We Touch Him: Practical Religious Experiences*, New York: Image Books, 1977.

Swift, Helen Cecilia, S.N.D. DEN., *Prayer for Sunset Years*, Cincinnati, OH: St. Anthony Messenger Press, 1986.

Magazines

Living Prayer, Gertrude Wilkinson and Mary Roman, ocd, editors, Barre, VT

Praying: Spirituality for Everyday Living, Art Winter, editor, The National Catholic Reporter Publishing Company, Inc., Kansas City, MO

Organizations

The following addresses and telephone numbers were taken from the Encyclopedia of Associations, Gale Research Inc., Detroit, 1993 Edition. It is available in most libraries.

Alcoholics Anonymous World Services
475 Riverside Drive
New York, NY 10163
212-686-1100

Alzheimer's Association
919 N. Michigan Ave. Ste. 1000
Chicago, IL 60611
800-621-0379

The American Association for Retired Persons
601 E Street, NW
Washington, DC 20049

American Cancer Society
1599 Clifton Rd. NE
Atlanta, GA 30329
800-ACS-2345

American Diabetes Association National Center
P.O. Box 25757 1660 Duke St.
Alexandria, VA 22314
800-232-3472

American Kidney Fund
6110 Executive Blvd., Ste. 1010
Rockville, MD 20852
800-638-8299

American Liver Foundation
1425 Pompton Ave.
Cedar Grove, NJ 07009
800-223-0179

The Beginning Experience Central Office
305 Michigan Avenue
Detroit, MI 48226
(313) 965-5110

Drugs Anonymous
P.O. Box 433 Ansonia Station
New York, NY 10023
212-874-0700

Gamblers Anonymous
3255 Wilshire Blvd. No. 610
Los Angeles, CA 90010
213-386-8789

National Council for Homemakers
Home Health Aide Services
1790 Broadway
New York, NY 10019

Overeaters Anonymous
P.O. Box 92870
Los Angeles, Ca 90009
213-618-8835

Sources and Acknowledgments

The following sources have been quoted in this book:

Addiction and Grace by Gerald May. HarperSanFrancisco, 1988.

The Addictive Organization by Anne Wilson Schaef and Diane Fassel. HarperSanFrancisco, 1990.

Anticipatory Grief by Schoenberg, Carr, Kutscher, Peretz, Goldberg. New York: Columbia University Press, 1974.

Codependent No More by Melody Beattie. New York: Harper/Hazelden, 1987.

The Dance of Intimacy by Harriet Goldhor Lerner. New York: Harper and Row, 1989.

The Healing of Codependence by Peter McCall, OFM Capuchin. Pecos, NM: Dove Publications, 1991.

Helping Children with the Mystery of Death by Elizabeth L. Reed. Nashville, TN: Abingdon Press, 1970.

Homecoming: Reclaiming and Championing Your Inner Child by John Bradshaw. New York: Bantam Books, 1990.

Living Through Personal Crisis by Ann Keiser Stearns. Chicago: Thomas More Press, 1984.

Prayerbook for Shabbat, Festivals and Weekdays. Edited with translation by Rabbi Jules Harlow. New York: The Rabbinical Assembly/United Synagogue of America.

"The Prayer of Tears" by Edward M. Hays. *Sign*, 1979.

Traits of a Healthy Family by Dolores Curran. HarperSan-Francisco, 1985.

Treasury of Jewish Quotations by Leo Rosten. New York: McGraw Hill, 1972.

You Can Be Real with God by Jim Scully. Pecos, NM: Dove Publications, 1992.

When Society Becomes an Addict by Anne Wilson Schaef. HarperSanFrancisco, 1987.

The quotes used at the beginning of these chapters were taken from the following sources:

Chapter 2: *The Singing: A Fable About What Makes Us Human* by Theron Raines. New York: The Atlantic Monthly Press, 1988.

Chapter 4: *Generation to Generation* by Edwin Friedman. New York: The Guilford Press, 1985.

Chapter 6: *Caring for Your Aged Parents* by Earl A. Grollman and Sharon H. Grollman. Boston: Beacon Press, 1978.

Chapter 7: *Learning to Say Goodbye: When a Parent Dies* by Eda LeShan. New York: Macmillan, 1976.

Chapter 8: *The Orphaned Adult* by Marc D. Angel. New York: Insight Books, Human Sciences Press, 1987.

Chapter 9: as quoted by Sean Caufield, *America*, February 29, 1992.